Finances out of co[ntrol]
a trip around the [world]
or a comfortable r[etirement]
can get a grip on [your finances]
investing to make [your money grow]

M000189085

Everybody needs help getting started, but who can you trust? A guide to investment advisers of all stripes, including financial planners, full-service brokers, investment clubs and discount brokers.

Stop burying your hard-earned cash in savings accounts! Here's the lowdown on stocks, bonds, mutual funds, life insurance, money market funds, gold and silver, collectibles and real estate.

They say, "different strokes for different folks," and that's especially true of investing. The experts reveal a host of investment strategies designed to fit different personalities and investment goals.

An informed investor is a successful investor. And this practical guide teaches beginning investors how to read stock quotations, ticker tapes, mutual fund quotations and annual reports, plus teaching other information-gathering skills.

HARLEQUIN ULTIMATE GUIDES™

What Savvy Investors Know That You Don't

Harlequin Books

TORONTO • NEW YORK • LONDON
AMSTERDAM • PARIS • SYDNEY • HAMBURG
STOCKHOLM • ATHENS • TOKYO • MILAN

ISBN 0-373-80514-4

WHAT SAVVY INVESTORS KNOW THAT YOU DON'T

Copyright © 1997 by TD Media Inc.

Designed by Tim Cooper of **Proteus Design**.

This edition published by arrangement with Harlequin Books S.A.

Printed in U.S.A.

TABLE OF CONTENTS

Introduction

Every woman knows that all important events in life require careful planning. Top of the list are weddings, anniversaries, bar mitzvahs, first-communion parties, graduations, coming-out parties, and proms.

I spent eight months planning my wedding, starting the morning after Richard proposed. I could've done it in three months without my mother's help, but that's another story. First, I did my research, thumbing through hundreds of bridal magazines, looking for just the right gowns for me and my bridesmaids. I was supposed to look like Vivien Leigh in my A-line silk and lace extravaganza with the plunging neckline. My bridesmaids' lime green taffeta gowns would render them suitably anonymous, so that there could be no question who was the star of the show: *Moi!* Next we interviewed halls, caterers and bands, dropping in on the Dubinsky affair to sample the stuffed mushroom caps; the Miller nuptials to check out the ice-carvings; and the Lurie bar mitzvah to hear yet another rendition of "Strangers in the Night." You get the picture.

My story is not unusual. No woman in her right mind would dream of going into an important event without proper planning, whether it's a social rite of passage or a presentation to a big client.

And any savvy investor knows that beginning an investment program is no different. If you want your dreams to come true, or maybe even exceed your wildest expectations, you've got to start planning for it now. When asked why some people find themselves at retirement age with no real nest egg, a well-known financial planner once said "no one ever plans to fail. They just fail to plan." Don't let this happen to you, start today!

And take heart, starting an investment program is a simple five-step program. That makes it a great deal easier than planning a wedding—especially if you leave my mother out of it.

IRA

CMX AMEX ¥ GNMA

YTD Jan 98 p 5 99.09 99.13
+22.1%

NYSE Sysco 34 1/2

CBT

$ TCBY 4 1/4

NASDAQ

£ PORK BELLIES
40,000 lbs -cents per lb.
CSCE 89.75 60.82 Feb 97

Soybean Oil Crude Decatur lb. .21 .22

Safwy 10s01 8.9 67 112 1/4

CHAPTER ONE

Where in the World Are You?

Trying to find the Radio Shack at a new multi-level mall can be a daunting task. You can take my husband, Richard's, approach and wander around aimlessly for half an hour until you bump into it, or you can find one of those handy directory kiosks with a floor plan of the mall. Usually there's a brightly colored arrow somewhere in the diagram that points to the words, YOU ARE HERE.

Unfortunately, when it comes to personal finances, there are no brightly lit arrows. You've got to find your own way. So, your first step is not to make a shopping list of can't-miss stocks and high yield bonds, but to see how much cash you've got in the kitty. In other words, you've got to find out WHERE YOU ARE NOW before you can begin your journey toward financial independence.

DETERMINING
YOUR NET WORTH

If you thought only rock stars and software magnates like Bill Gates had assets worth totaling up, you might be in for a nice surprise. Many of us are worth quite a bit more than we think.

Even so, you might ask, why is it important to know your net worth? Savvy investors know that your net worth is a very useful snapshot of your financial status. It shows whether or not you have the wherewithal to get where you want to go in life. And on a more sober note, your net worth is also an indication of your ability to deal with a financial setback such as a business failure or the loss of a job.

Ready to begin? Okay, grab a pencil and some paper and let's get started. A sample chart is shown on the opposite page.

First, make a list of all your assets. This list will include the cash in your checking account, savings account, money market account, retirement plans, mutual funds, any individual stocks or bonds you might

Find Out What You're Worth

1. ADD UP WHAT YOU OWN (YOUR ASSETS)

	Typical Case	Your Assets
Savings Account	$7,500	
401K	$32,500	
Individual Retirement Acct.	$6,000	
Value of Home	$100,000	
Pension Benefits ($500 per month based on 15 years)	$75,000	
Total:	$221,000	

2. ADD UP WHAT YOU OWE (YOUR LIABILITIES)

	Typical Case	Your Liabilities
Credit Card Balance	$2,000	
Student Loans	$4,500	
Auto Loan	$10,000	
Mortgage Debt	$75,000	
Home Equity Loan	$5,000	
Total	$96,500	

3. FINDING YOUR NET WORTH

	Typical Case	Your Net Worth
Total Assets	$221,000	
(Minus) Total Liabilities	$96,500	
Net Worth	$124,500	

currently own, real estate, and the equity in your home or apartment. Total it up and get a fresh sheet of paper.

Next, list your liabilities, and I'm not talking about your chronically slow metabolism. By liabilities I mean everything you owe, including educational loans, first and second mortgages, credit card debt, and automobile loans.

Once you're sure you haven't left anything out, subtract your liabilities from your assets. The result is your net worth.

If you discover you're worth a lot less than you expected, don't be disheartened; you've just taken the first step to make your net worth grow.

Goal Setting

Now that you've done a little hard work, you get to reward yourself with a little constructive daydreaming. What kind of life would you like to have in ten years? Or twenty years from now? Is your dream a cottage in the South of France? A retirement condo on Hilton Head? A zippy red convertible? Or maybe it's putting that little genius of yours through Harvard and then medical school.

Whatever your dreams, they'll remain just dreams unless you figure out how much they'll cost and start making plans to make those dreams a reality.

So, gather all your real estate, college and travel brochures and sharpen those pencils again. It's time to do some serious figuring.

GOAL: A COMFORTABLE RETIREMENT

Experts agree that when figuring how much you'll need to retire on, you should plan on needing around 75 percent of your current living expenses. They're assuming that you'll be living somewhere such as Florida where the cost of living is lower, and you won't have the expenses of taking care of a family. But don't forget to factor in the cost of inflation. A good rule of thumb is to add an additional 6 percent for each year until you take off for Valhalla Golf Community.

Don't get out the calculator and start multiplying 6 percent times itself for every year until retirement. Financial advisors have figured out a simple number, called the inflation multiplier, that figures it out in one step. To adjust for inflation if your retirement is in five years, multiply your needed income by 1.2. For retirement in 10 years, multiply by 1.5. For retirement in 15 years, multiply by 1.8. For retirement in 20 years, multiply by 2.2.

Want to know how long you'll be needing that annual income? A male reaching the retirement age of 65 is likely to live another 15 years; a woman is likely to live another 19 years. A woman spending $75,000 a year would need $3.3 million dollars to get through her retirement 20 years from now.

But don't despair. A financial investor knows how small monthly payments, invested wisely, quickly add up to millions, thanks to the miracle of compound interest—the interest paid on interest you've already earned. More on that in a minute. Take Step Two toward financial independence: Figure out what you'll need to retire on the next page.

Figure Out What You Need to Retire

1. WHAT YOU NEED IN TODAY'S DOLLARS

	Typical Case	Your Retirement Needs
Current Annual Expenses	$75,000	
	x .75	x .75
Yearly income needed in today's dollars	$56,250	

2. WHAT YOU'LL NEED IN TOMORROW'S (INFLATED) DOLLARS

	Typical Case	Your Retirement Needs
Basic Annual Need	$56,250	
Inflation multiplier*	x 2.2	
*Choose your correct multiplier: (For retirement in 5 years enter 1.2) (For retirement in 10 years, enter 1.5) (For retirement in 15 years, enter 1.8) (For retirement in 20 years, enter 2.2)		
Yearly income needed in tomorrow's dollars	$123,750	

Where Does the Money Go?

SOLVING THE MYSTERY OF CASH FLOW

Ever hear about someone being "land poor" or "not being liquid"? Both of these are just fancy expressions for not being able to put your hands on a dollar when you need it because your assets are all tied up in investments—a house bigger than you can really afford or business inventory that you haven't sold. In business, this is called a cash flow problem. Without ready cash, a business can quickly grind to a halt, regardless of how well it's doing on the balance sheet.

And it's no different for you and your future.

So, how do you determine your family's cash flow?

Once again, you don't need a team of economists and a mainframe computer. Everything you need will probably be in the top drawer of your desk or wherever you toss the monthly bills until it's time to pay them. So pull open that drawer. Grab your pay stubs, credit card statements, canceled checks, and any other monthly bills. And don't forget your ATM slips!

First, add up all of your monthly income after taxes. This will include your take-home pay from work, real estate income if you own rental property, and any dividends or other income you receive on a regular basis.

Next add up all your bills and regular expenses and subtract the total from your monthly income. *Violà* a snapshot of your monthly cash flow. If you're disciplined, there'll probably be something left over to

Where Does the Money Go?

FIRST, FIGURE OUT YOUR INCOME		
	Sample Case	**Your Cash Flow**
Pay Stub (after taxes)	$3,125	
Rent Income		
Dividends		
Your Income	**$3,125**	

THEN FIGURE OUT YOUR EXPENSES		
	Sample Case	**Your Expenses**
Rent or Mortgage	$800	
Gas/Electric	$100	
Water	$20	
Phone	$50	
Cable	$40	
Grocery Bills	$475	
Restaurants	$125	
Gasoline	$40	
Parking	$20	
Auto Loan	$336	
Credit Card	$200	
Student Loan	$150	
Clothing	$100	
Shoes	$20	
Dry Cleaning/Laundry	$50	

continued on next page

	Sample Case	Your Expenses
Charity/Religious	$150	
Life Insurance	$75	
Auto Insurance	$50	
Health Insurance	$100	
Books/Magazines	$50	
Doctor/Dentist	$25	
Entertainment (videos, movies etc.)	$75	
Total Expenses	$3,051	

set aside for the future, including your new investment program.

But if you're like me, you'll discover not only that your standard of living has risen to meet your income over the years, but has actually exceeded it!

JUST WHEN YOU THOUGHT IT WAS SAFE TO GO BACK TO THE ATM...

Okay, that wasn't so bad was it? Maybe it's not a pretty picture, but you're still covering your expenses with a little bit left over. Maybe you can start that investment program after all, right?

Don't be so hasty. If you're like me, you've left out a few very important items that don't occur monthly, but rather annually—things that could push your financial statement into the red.

To spare you any further suspense, I'm talking about Christmas, summer vacations, birthdays, and anniversaries. If you've got a large family like my husband, the holiday season is a major cash drain. When we go to Florida to see his folks, that's $2,500 counting airfares and presents. How about birthdays? In our neighborhood, no kid is content with a cake and couple of friends over to wish him or her well. Now, throw in an additional $1,000 for a brief family vacation in the summer.

Using just these three examples, there's probably an extra $4,000 a year, or $333 a month that needs to be accounted for. More than enough to destroy our sample budget.

So, get back to the drawing board and do a second pass at your family cash flow snapshot.

Plug The Leaks

SAVE, SAVE, SAVE

When you're living beyond your means, you've only got two choices: make more money or use the "B" word—budget.

Doing a budget is like doing your makeup under harsh fluorescent light—a shock. You see all the little so-called "laugh lines" and all the blemishes. When I first did our budget five years ago, I discovered that when it came to handling money, the Smiths, far from being a practical, sober American family full of old-fashioned values, were actually no better than sailors blowing into port after six months at sea. Eating out and video rentals had somehow grown from occasional treats to inalienable rights protected by Congress, the Supreme Court and the Federal Reserve.

At the rate our money was flying out the door, we'd have run through our savings in another six months. "Smith Inc." had a negative cash flow, so there was no way we could possibly start an investment program without making some budgetary cuts, and fast!

RIGHTSIZING YOUR MONTHLY BUDGET

Do you have any idea how much you're spending each month for convenience?

If you're like most people, you could cut anywhere from a hundred to five hundred dollars a month from your expenses if you trimmed some of the goods and services that your parents would've considered luxuries, but that you've become accustomed to. How to cut? Take a page from the giant corporations and downsize!

The first thing on my list five years ago was the lawn service. We live in a neighborhood full of urban refugees, urbanites who migrated from Brooklyn after World War II. They're mystified by green lawns and flowers that grow out of the ground instead of window boxes, and so they have no tradition of cutting their own lawns or cleaning their own gutters. Those are things "the guy" does, as in "Honey, the gutters are full of pine needles. Call the guy."

Well, I called "the guy" all right, and told him that since my husband was now working out of the house that he would be cutting the lawn from now on. Bingo! One hundred dollars a month.

Next I restructured our entertainment division, giving the boot to premium cable, and putting a strict limit on movie and video game rentals, cutting our monthly outflow by another fifty dollars.

Okay, my life and your life are different, but everyone has some things they can trim from their budget in order to prepare for the future. And if you think a couple hundred bucks a month is nothing, think again. It's $2,400 a year. Even if you never increased the amount, $2,400 just sitting in a bank account earns interest. And the interest earns interest. If the account earns 6 percent interest, your annual deposit of $2,400 has grown to $95,982 by the time you're ready to retire 20 years from now.

GRANDPA SMITH'S TREASURE CHEST

My father-in-law is a classic child of the depression, raised in a time when jobs and money were scarce. Even though he was a modestly paid Protestant minister until he retired a few years ago, he managed to build a very impressive stock portfolio over the years—all by watching pennies and investing. One of his favorite tricks was to shop sales at the local drug store and stock up on shaving cream, razor blades, toothpaste, toothbrushes, deodorant, and ballpoint pens among other things. Then he'd lock away his treasure in an old footlocker until someone in the family needed something. Then, according to my husband, you'd accompany Reverend Smith upstairs to unlock the treasure chest.

Grandpa Smith also bought a big freezer and installed it on the back porch so that he could buy day-old bread, a large quantity of meat from a wholesale butcher, and poultry on sale.

A bit extreme? Perhaps, but his five children never wanted for anything while growing up, and now the senior Smiths are enjoying a comfortable retirement in Florida and have made half a dozen trips to Europe in the past ten years. Oh yes, and even though his five children have long since left home, Grandpa Smith still invests regularly and watches his pennies.

His favorite strategy these days is buying in bulk from Sam's Club, the discounter in his area. Grandpa Smith claims he saves between 30 and 40 percent off the retail cost of household items such as toilet paper, paper towels, and chicken nuggets (one of Grandpa's favorites)—a claim I can back up from my own experience at the local discounter, PriceCostco.

If you don't belong to one of these wholesale discounters, I strongly urge you to look into it. It's a great start for freeing up dollars to invest toward your goals.

Now What???

Reality Check

If after doing all these exercises you're still having trouble locating enough cash to invest, take a tip from my brother Raymond, a corporate consultant: "Map out your process." Ray specializes in showing corporations that what they think they're doing and what they're actually doing are often two different things.

The same thing is often true of family finances. All of us are guilty of wasting money without realizing it, but the only way to find out for sure is keep a detailed record of everything you spend for a month. Everything? Yes, everything, right down to the quarter you put in the parking meter when you go to your favorite fitness club.

At the end of the month, you'll find some interesting surprises—things you would never have put in the family budget. Like three visits to Toys "R" Us to buy your kids yet another action hero they just had to have—even though their bedrooms are filled with toys they never look at. Like going out for lunch at work at $10 a pop when a bag lunch would save you between $30 and $40 a week. And what about those impulse buys at the grocery store that not only add up to wasted money, but extra inches at the end of the year! Get the picture? Then get yourself a pocket-sized notebook and be vigilant.

A WORD ABOUT SAVINGS

My brother Raymond is fond of telling his corporate customers that "you can't save your way to profitability," meaning that merely cutting jobs and closing plants will not in and of itself make a company

SAVE MONEY

Ten Easy Tips for Cutting Your Monthly Spending

1. Pay cash for everything.

2. Join a discount wholesaler.

3. Drastically curtail your use of credit cards.

4. Use coupons.

5. Take your lunch to work.

6. Stock up on basics when they're on sale.

7. Cut out impulse buying.

8. Reduce tobacco and alcohol consumption.

9. Shop around for lower insurance rates.

10. Have your doctor prescribe generic drugs.

financially healthy. To do that, you've got to grow revenues and profits.

A DAILY FINANCIAL DIARY

Coffee and Donut	$2.00
Newspaper	$.50
Deli Lunch	$10.00
Vending Machine Drink	$1.00
New Pair of Hose	$4.00
Birthday Gift	$20.00
Stamps	$20.00
Gum	$.60
Glue to fix broken vase	$1.50
Total	$59.60

The same thing is true of personal finances. Merely cutting your spending won't get you on that cruise to Hawaii, but it is a critical first step toward accomplishing your goals. Beginning to save, whether it's 5 percent, 10 percent or 20 percent of your income, is the only way to learn to live within your means. Once you've accomplished that, you will have stopped the monthly bleeding, introduced financial discipline into your life, and created a war chest of money to invest for your future. Then you, too, will be in a position to grow revenues and profits, just like the big boys.

WHO ARE YOU?

Okay, now you've got your bankroll, and it's burning a hole in your pocket, right? Some of you are consumed with the urge to bury it in the backyard, and others have their eyes on the toaster oven that your friendly savings & loan will give you for opening an account, while still others of you are just dying to run down to the nearest stock broker and plunk it all down on Netscape, Waste Management or whatever the hot stock of the moment is.

Sound vaguely familiar? Well, it's right out of the New Testament—the parable of the three servants who were given a portion of their master's wealth to take care of while he was away on a trip. One of them literally buried his talent in the ground, while another lent it out for modest interest, while the third presumably took a little risk and managed to double his master's money.

Now, I'm not saying that it's a religious experience to invest in the stock market, but the simple truth is that historically it's the best way to grow wealth. While there's an element of risk in investing, it's not the same thing as sidling up to a paramutual window and putting $10 on the nose of Easy Riches. At the same time, however, it's not for everybody. Don't get me wrong. I firmly believe that nearly everyone has the potential to be a successful investor, but you've got to be willing to do a modest amount of work on a regular basis.

So, go to your bathroom mirror and ask yourself the following question, "Am I willing to do the few hours a week that's required, without fail?" A little overly dramatic? Perhaps, but this may be the most important step you take in your bid for financial independence.

Chances are if you have taken all the steps in the program thus far, you've got what it takes to be a successful investor. However, if you really don't feel that you

A PENNY SAVED IS A PENNY EARNED

How Compound Interest Makes $2,400 Grow

Invest $2,400 at	6%	8%	10%
Value in 5 Years	$3,212	$3,526	$3,865
Value in 10 Years	$4,298	$5,181	$6,225
Value in 15 Years	$5,752	$7,613	$10,025
Value in 20 Years	$7,697	$11,186	$16,146

can commit the time, take your hard-earned stash down to the bank and open up a money market account. If you stick to your program of setting something aside each month, you'll still have the satisfaction of a savings program and the knowledge that you're making considerable progress toward realizing your dreams. And that, my friend, is all there is to this last step—invest what you've saved. The above chart shows what $2,400 would be worth if you invested it for various lengths of time at various rates. But don't forget, your goal isn't to invest $2,400. It's to invest $2,400 each year. And remember: $2,400 invested annually at 6 percent will be worth $95,982 when you retire in 20 years.

CHAPTER TWO

Who To Invest With

HOW TO FIND
A FINANCIAL ADVISOR

Professional help is a necessity when starting an investment program for a couple of reasons. First, there's a bewildering number of options when it comes time to actually invest the money you've worked so hard to save. Second, you can't just waltz down the aisle of a financial supermarket and pull a few shares of General Motors off the shelves—at least not yet. In most cases, you still need a pro to purchase the stock or bond for you, whether it's in individual units or through a mutual fund.

Financial professionals are a combination of personal shopper, high school guidance counselor, and aluminum siding salesman. They can be your best friends or your worst enemies. So, how do you find the right one? The same way you find a mate—by looking *very* carefully.

Like most of the men you've dated while looking for Mr. Right, financial advisors are not knights in shining armor who have only your best interests at heart. They're professionals who make their livings selling you either their time or a specific set of financial products. Don't get me wrong. Many of them are decent, hard-working men and women who really do want to do a good job for you, but you have to do your homework.

To make your job that much harder, everyone—including insurance agents, accountants, stock brokers, and part-time tax preparers—seems to be hanging out their shingles and calling themselves "financial advisors" these days. Consequently, you'll probably make several stops while out shopping for services depending on your particular needs and goals. So, in this section we'll be looking at the various kinds of financial professionals and showing you the advantages and disadvantages of each type.

Before you hand over your hard-earned money to anyone to invest, you'd better do your homework. How should you begin? Whatever you do, don't run to the phone book to look up financial advisors or investment counselors unless you're new in your area and don't know anyone. Start with your personal network.

Ask your friends, neighbors, and relatives for recommendations. Once the word gets out, they'll only be too happy to help, but don't take everything you hear as gospel. Press them for details. Ask them what kind of return they've gotten on their investments, and whether they're happy with the service they've received. If they get vague when you ask for more information or simply can't tell you why they like a particular broker or investment advisor, you probably can cross that name off your list, or at least downgrade it to *questionable*.

A word of caution: even if your friends swear by their advisors and regale you with thrilling tales of making a killing in the market, take it with a grain of salt.

When it comes to love or money, people have a way of exaggerating their successes and forgetting their failures. Let me give you an example.

At my cousin Mindy's wedding (her third), my Uncle Max from the Flatbush side of the family sidled up to me with a conspiratorial look in his eye. Then with his mouth full of crackers and chopped liver, Uncle Max whispered, "Garbage." It turns out that Uncle Max's broker had gotten him into Waste Management, an environmental clean-up and recycling firm, when it was selling for a song. Ever since, "garbage" has been Uncle Max's investment mantra, and his broker has been his god. What Uncle Max didn't tell me was how the same broker got him slaughtered when he suggested speculating in pork bellies (yeecch!) and betting big on biotechnology stocks. According to Aunt Anita (my inside source), this is why they still live in a third floor walk-up in Brooklyn.

PROFESSIONAL COURTESY, OR THICK AS THIEVES?

Another word of caution. Unfortunately, recommendations are not always what they seem. Let's say you ring up Jake, the lawyer who handled the closing on your house and your will. You figure that with all his money that Jake will know a really top-notch investment counselor. And he may. The problem is that some professionals have informal agreements to send each other clients. If the agreement is based on a genuine respect for each other's professional skills, then there's no harm done. All too often, however, Jake the lawyer has no idea whether Bob the investment counselor is any good at what he does. So proceed cautiously with professional recommendations.

GET UP CLOSE AND PERSONAL

Now that you've gotten two gilt-edged recommendations from Uncle Max and Jake the lawyer, your work has just begun. As

INVESTMENT TIP #1

HOW TO CHECK UP
ON YOUR BROKER

You've got a short list of potential brokers, but don't know which one to choose. For a tie-breaker, get some background information on their firms through the National Association of Securities Dealers or from the Central Registration Depository files which you can get from your state securities agency. Write or call either association and they'd be happy to help you.

National Association of
Securities Dealers:
1735 K Street, N.W.,
Washington, DC, 20006-1506
(800) 289-9999.

State Securities Regulator:
North American Securities
Administrators Association,
1 Massachusetts Ave., N.W.,
Suite 310,
Washington, DC, 20001
(202) 737-0900.

INVESTMENT TIP #2

PROTECT YOURSELF WITH GOOD RECORDS

To protect yourself against future problems with your financial advisor or broker, get everything that passes between you down on paper or on audio tape.

The law requires you to inform anyone whose conversation you are recording, so be scrupulous about doing so. Besides, the knowledge that conversations are being recorded has the wonderful effect of keeping people on the up-and-up in the first place.

Mindy's second husband, the Volvo dealer, used to say, "it's time to qualify the customer," by which he meant "let's find out if these folks can make the monthly payments." In the case of financial professionals, it means finding out whether they can do the job for you.

The easiest way to do that is with a personal interview. Call them up and ask for a few minutes of their time. Explain that they were recommended by your Uncle Max or whomever, and that you're looking for a financial advisor. If they're too busy to grant a personal interview, you probably can cross their names off your list. Phone interviews, in my experience, don't cut it. You can't watch her eyes to see if she is really paying attention, and you can't see whether she's got a gravy stain on her suit. Most important, though, even if she is the greatest broker in the world, she can't do you any good if she doesn't know your goals and your philosophy—things that are difficult to talk about without a personal interview.

On the next page, I've listed ten questions you should ask your prospective advisor during an interview. They'll give you something to talk about during those awkward "getting to know you" moments, and more important, your prospective advisor's answers will give you a basis for comparison with other candidates. So, don't forget to take notes!

TEN KEY QUESTIONS TO ASK A PROSPECTIVE FINANCIAL ADVISOR

1. What's your investment philosophy?

2. How do you invest your own money?

3. What formal training have you had that qualifies you as a financial advisor?

4. How many years of experience have you had?

5. Can you give me some names of satisfied clients with goals and finances similar to mine?

6. Do you make your money from commissions, fees, or both?

7. What are your fees?

8. Are you independent or do you work for a brokerage firm or insurance company?

9. Do they require you to represent any particular product line?

10. Do you carry professional liability insurance?

THE INTERVIEW

A good interview is always a two-way street. The questions your prospective advisor asks you are just as important as the ones you've posed for him or her. For example, was he interested in the details of your situation? Did he or she ask about your financial and personal goals? What about your investment philosophy? Your attitude toward risk?

If your candidate is interested in compiling a balanced profile on you, then you might have a winner. But watch out for the following danger signals. Number one: The prospective advisor immediately moves into a selling mode, pitching high commission products such as annuities or limited partnerships. Number two: The prospective advisor emphasizes the difficulties of investing, and suggests an arrangement in which he or she will manage your assets for a fee.

Basically, you should be wary of anyone who tries to sell you anything without fully understanding the details of your situation. When this happens, it almost invariably means that the prospective advisor is pushing products based on the commissions he or she receives, and not on whether they fit your needs.

Getting Past the Credentials

SEARCHING FOR THE RIGHT ONE

Now that you've interviewed two or three prospective financial advisors, you've probably noticed that they all have fancy initials after their names like RIA (Registered Investment Advisor) or CFP (Certified Financial Planner). And they might tell you that they're members of impressive sounding organizations, like the International Association of Financial

Planners (IAFP) or the Institute of Certified Financial Planners (ICFP).

Should you be impressed? Absolutely not. At present, financial planning is basically an *unregulated* profession. Even though the professional associations provide workshops and other training, like most trade associations they exist to promote the welfare of their members, *not their members' clients*. The simple fact is that in most places all you need to do to become a financial planner is to declare yourself one.

THE FULL-SERVICE BROKER

We've all seen those expensive television ads promoting Wall Street brokerage houses. You know, the ones with smug, well-dressed people enjoying golden retirements while classical music plays softly in the background? They always attribute their success to their good personal friend down at Paine Webber, Merrill Lynch, Smith Barney or wherever.

These good personal friends are full-service brokers, and they're not friends for free. When you work with a full-service broker, every time you buy stock or other securities, it will cost you approximately three to five percent of the trade in commissions. Look at it this way: If you have $1,000 to invest, it could cost you as much as $50 to do it through a full-service broker. So instead of having a grand to invest, you now only have $950. And when you sell your shares, they'll charge you another three to five percent on the full value of the stock. If you've made money, the

 INVESTMENT TIP #3

RIA—Away!

Beware of people using the letters RIA after their name. The Securities Exchange Commission requires everyone who is giving investment advice to register with them. Afterwards they are called Registered Investment Advisors. This is not a credential, however, and should never be used on business cards or letterheads.

return on your initial investment will be that much smaller. If your investment has dropped in value since you bought it, you'll not only take the loss, but end up paying your broker an additional three to five percent for the pleasure.

If your good personal friend, the broker, supplies you with valuable market advice, maybe the commissions are worth it. That's something only you can decide. Keep in mind, however, that commissions are the only way full-service brokers make money, so they have a big incentive to make sure you're an active trader.

THE OTHER SIDE OF THE COIN: THE SERVICES OFFERED BY FULL-SERVICE BROKERS

Since the securities industry was deregulated in 1974, full-service brokers have been in a fiercely competitive battle with discount brokers who offer better commission rates. Yet despite the higher cost, the full-service broker can still be an incredibly valuable ally.

First of all, full-service brokers provide a tremendous range of services. They spend time with individual clients giving them professional advice and counsel. They hold securities so that clients do not need to take possession of them, making trading easier and faster when it's time to sell. They offer asset management accounts, in which the brokerage manages your money, including making stock trades, in exchange for an annual fee. They also provide detailed monthly statements of account activity, and they provide you with information from the companies you've invested in.

Most important, however, the full-service broker is a fount of ready information. Full-service brokers can provide you with Value Line surveys (the single most valuable piece of research you can get on most companies), investment newsletters, Standard & Poor reports, stock prospectuses, annual and quarterly reports, ownership data, reports on insider buying, and much more.

Can you get all of this information

yourself? Certainly, but at a considerable cost in your time. The question is, is it worth the extra 30 cents a share above the rate a discount broker would charge? Only you can decide.

THE DISCOUNT BROKER

You've also seen ads on television for discount brokers, outfits like Charles Schwab and Quick & Reilly. They promise to make trading a lot easier and cheaper, and for people who know what they want to buy, it makes a lot of sense. You call them up, and they make your trades for you for significantly less than the full-service brokerage houses. What's more, the discount broker doesn't have a line of products to sell like many full-service houses, so there's no conflict of interest or tempting sales pitches for you to worry about. Most important, at the end of the day, you get to keep more of your money when you invest and more of your profits when you sell. Sounds like a great deal, right? Yes, it does, except for a couple of little things.

COMMISSION COMPARISON

For 100 shares of Stock Listed at $40

Brokerage Type	Commission
Full-Service Broker	$120-$200
Discount Broker	$56-$82
Deep-Discount Broker	$29-$35

If you're a neophyte investor, you need to be careful on two counts. Number one: discount brokers do not offer advice; they just execute trades. So unless you're getting great advice from someone else, a discount broker might not be the best option for you. Number two: discount houses typically have minimum charges to keep your account active. If you're a small investor making relatively few trades, you run the danger of having any possible savings eaten up in minimum charges. The bottom line: unless you do your homework, you could end up not saving any money and getting no guidance to boot!

DEEP-DISCOUNT BROKERS

Despite what you might think, deep-discount brokers are not people who sell you securities in the dark recesses of parking garages. They differ from discount brokers only in that their commission structure is even more favorable to the customer than the first generation of discount brokers such as Charles Schwab.

Increasingly, deep-discount brokers are people you might never meet at all, since a growing portion of their business is done over touch-tone telephone or over the Internet. In fact, many deep-discount brokers offer you additional savings of up to 10 percent, if you're able to execute your trades over the phone or by computer.

Needless to say, before you go running

into any broker's outstretched arms, you
need to look closely at their minimum
charges and services they offer.

More About Conflicts of Interest

LET THE BUYER BEWARE

Savvy investors realize that approximately 90 percent of all financial advisors make their money off commissions and that these commissions come out of the principal that you're investing with them. This is true regardless of whether they're selling life insurance, stocks, bonds, or mutual funds. Furthermore, the rate of commission varies from investment to investment, so your financial advisor has an incentive to sell you one product over another, regardless of its benefit to you.

These fundamental conflicts of interest should make you a little wary of following any advisor's suggestions blindly.

DOUBLE-DIPPING: THE NEXT-TO-WORST-CASE SCENARIO

Now that you realize that if your friendly financial professional isn't charging you an hourly fee, he's making commissions on what he sells you, everything is out in the open, right? Unfortunately, there's more that you need to be concerned with. Even if you are being charged a fee for services, some advisors have been known to also collect commissions on the products they sell you—a practice known as double-dipping. And in both cases, you're the one who's paying!

If you're still confused on this subject, it helps to lump all people who make their money on commissions, whether they're dealing in automobiles, insurance, or stocks and bonds as salespeople—they make money based on what you spend.

CHURNING:
THE WORST-CASE SCENARIO

My mother thinks "churn" is something you make butter in, while my husband thinks it's something out of *Jaws*—a bucket of fish parts thrown into the water to attract sharks. Mom's butter churn conjures up an image of something being constantly stirred, while Richard's suggests a feeding frenzy by ravenous beasts.

In a way they're both right.

Churning is where a greedy broker or financial planner executes a high number of trades for your account, thereby turning it over or stirring it, in order to generate commissions and fees for himself.

If you question them about the volume of trading in your account, they'll give you plenty of reasons why it needed to be done. They'll talk about market trends, Federal Reserve data about the economy, and events in the companies you've invested in. At the end of the day, however, your account will be eaten up by commissions, and the brokers will be the only ones making money.

INVESTMENT TIP #4

HOW TO KNOW WHEN YOUR ACCOUNT IS BEING CHURNED

If you suspect your broker is trading too often in order to generate commissions for himself, take a close look at your brokerage statement. Experts say a good rule of thumb is that if your broker's commissions add up to 10 percent of the total value of your account, you're probably being churned.

Protecting yourself against "churn" and broker fraud

The easiest way to protect yourself from "churn" or excessive trading in your account is not to authorize a discretionary brokerage account in the first place.

If you really feel the need for someone to manage your portfolio at that level, then make sure your financial advisor does not work on commission, so there will be no incentive to churn your account, or limit your investments to low-load (low-fee) mutual funds.

Experts also suggest sending a letter to the brokerage house when you open your account explaining in clear language what your investment goals are, how much risk you are willing to take, and a snapshot of your financial status. With such a letter on file, it will be very difficult for a broker to *misunderstand* your intentions and engage in unauthorized trading in order to generate commissions.

You should also read any statements from the brokerage firm as soon as you get them. Read them carefully, looking for signs of trades you didn't originate, and unusual fees charged to your account. Keeping a careful watch over your account is still the best way to nip any unauthorized activity in the bud.

TELEPHONE SALES: THE BLIND DATE OF THE INVESTMENT WORLD

How many blind dates have you ever had that worked out? "He's a real nice guy with a

> ## INVESTMENT TIP #5

TELEPHONE TIPS

This can't be stressed too many times. Never buy securities, diamonds, land or anything else based on a telephone solicitation, especially if it comes from someone you don't know. If what they were offering were such a great deal, believe me, they wouldn't be calling.

great sense of humor," always meant that your date would be as homely as a bedpost and a "Three Stooges" fan. You should be equally wary of investments pitched to you over the telephone by people you don't know, regardless of how well-known their employer might be.

Telephone solicitations are normally conducted out of large rooms full of people at telephones. Every so often they are given lists of products that the brokerage wants them to sell, and in some outfits they are given carefully worded scripts to help the salesmen move the stock.

Look at it this way. If Consolidated Tennis Bracelets is such a great buy, why are they calling you? Shouldn't they want to keep as much of this stock for themselves or their top customers as possible? Wall Street insiders do not get incredibly wealthy by sharing with the average person. When a hot new stock first comes on the market (known as the IPO, or initial public offering), the insiders who hold the stock for the first few hours and days make the big killings. You probably won't hear about it for weeks or months, and even then, it probably won't be through a telephone solicitation.

So the next time you get an unsolicited call pitching "an incredible deal" on a stock, just say no.

IF IT SOUNDS TOO GOOD TO BE TRUE, IT PROBABLY IS...

If your advisor or anyone else ever pitches you a stock or a limited partnership deal that will return 40-50 percent on your

INVESTMENT TIP #6

When Breaking Up is Hard To Do

Okay, you've caught your broker churning your account, or more likely, you're just not getting the kind of results you'd like. You desperately want out, but don't like scenes. What should you do? You could send him a note explaining why you need a change, but unless your broker is your brother-in-law, you probably don't owe him an explanation. The easiest thing to do is to hire another broker and let him take care of the necessary details.

investment, take to the hills! Admittedly, there's a very small chance that the investment could really be that good, but the chance is so small that it's not worth taking.

Even though the stock market has been very kind to investors over the last decade, the average return has only been about 15 percent annually. If you look at performance since the 1920s, the average return has been around 10 percent. Naturally, there have been individual mutual funds and stocks that have outperformed the market, but it's foolhardy to believe that anyone can guarantee you high returns. Either they're not telling you about the inordinately high risks you would be taking if you invest, or they're simply overstating the prospects of the investment.

SHOPPING FOR SERVICES AMONG DISCOUNT BROKERS

Full-service brokerages aren't the only ones that offer services. If you're willing to shop around, you could find a discount broker that will not only give you a considerable break on commissions, but will also offer you some valuable services. However, be careful not to buy services that don't fit your immediate needs. Here are just a few of the most popular services.

If you're a big player, or expect to become one some day, you might be inter-

INVESTMENT TIP #7

WATCH OUT FOR SURCHARGES

While checking out discounts, check into surcharges that some firms levy on stocks priced below $5 a share, or for trading in odd lots, which the industry defines as anything less than groups of 100 shares.

ested in Securities Investor Protection Corporation (SIPC) coverage for your account. While SIPC insurance doesn't protect you against failures in the market, it does protect you against the failure of the brokerage. The organization insures the holdings in individual accounts up to $500,000 including up to $100,000 in cash and its equivalents. However, many brokerage houses buy additional coverage for their big customers, some at no additional charge to you.

Everyone who has a brokerage account carries a cash balance at some time or another, usually from selling a portion of their portfolio. The question is, what happens to that money before it's reinvested? Savvy investors expect it to earn interest, and look for a brokerage house that not only pays interest but automatically places their cash in money market funds until they're ready to reinvest them.

Self-directed Individual Retirement Accounts (IRAs) are also a service that most firms offer these days. These allow the individuals to put their retirement savings in stocks and bonds instead of depositing cash in the local bank's IRA. The attraction of IRAs is that they let you accumulate value tax-free until you begin withdrawals at retirement age, when you will presumably be taxed at a lower rate. But the self-directed IRA gives you the added advantage of letting you invest in the stock market (if you so choose) while avoiding the heavy capital-gains taxes on your successful stock trades.

Since prices for this service vary, you should shop around if you're interested in a self-directed IRA.

INVESTMENT CLUBS

If you "play well with others," as elementary school teachers put it, then you might want to investigate joining, or even starting, an investment club. For the novice, investment clubs offer several advantages. First of all, they're more social than investing all by your lonesome, and learning something new is often easier when done in the company of others. Second, members of investment clubs usually contribute a modest amount each month—anywhere from $25 to $100—making it a low-cost way to learn about investing. The resulting pool makes it possible to invest in stocks that you couldn't afford otherwise. Third, the work of researching individual stocks and bonds is spread around the group, making the whole process easier for everyone.

To learn more about investment clubs, contact the following organization.

**NATIONAL ASSOCIATION OF
INVESTORS CORPORATION**
711 W. Thirteen-Mile Road
Madison Heights, MI 48071
(810) 583-6242

TAKE THE MIDDLE ROAD

If after reading this chapter you're a little wary of trusting financial advisors, then I say, "Good." It's a healthy state to be in when looking for financial help. But if you're discouraged about the entire process, don't be. There's somebody out there just right for you, maybe even two somebodies! Let me explain.

When I was in the market for an advisor, I collected a pocketful of business cards, and even interviewed two or three candidates including my Uncle Max's broker, the "genius of Flatbush" Harold Lefkowitz. Harold had soup stains on his tie (one of my personal warning signals) and spent most of our time together talking about getting me into the "lucrative" commodities market. I knew right away we'd never be an item. Unfortunately, my interviews with the other candidates weren't much better. But just when I was about to get discouraged, my cousin Mindy told me about Jack Tate. As it turned out, Jack was a financial planner, and the coach of her son's Little League team.

What made me want to meet him was the fact that Jack's team was next to last in the standings, but all the kids had a great time. Apparently Jack was more interested in making sure all the kids got a chance to play than he was in winning games.

Mindy introduced me to Jack at the next game, and the three of us went out for coffee afterwards. As soon as the coffee arrived, I hit Jack with my ten questions. Mindy was horrified, but Jack took it all in stride and gave me the answers I was looking for. Just as I figured, he was a good listener and wanted to help me do what I wanted to do on my terms. After coffee, Jack agreed to work with me as a fee-based planner, charging me by the hour for his services, and agreed to accept my condition that I would buy no products from him. In gratitude, I picked up the tab.

With Jack's help, I hooked up with an excellent discount broker in New York. Their minimums were low enough so that even as a small investor I still saved money over the big brokerage houses. Furthermore, the discount broker offered me no-load (no commission) mutual funds with a good track record as an additional service. So, for the price of a frozen cappuccino, I picked up not only an advisor I could trust, but ultimately a discount broker who gives me not only good prices, but also the services I really need.

CHAPTER THREE

Where To Invest Your Capital

WALL STREET

When I started my investment program five years ago, I didn't know the difference between a zero-coupon bond and a coupon for 25 cents off the price of peanut butter. The first time I met with my financial advisor, I was pretty confused when he started talking about common stocks, treasuries, no-loads, annuities, and other investments. I nodded as though I knew what he was talking about and scribbled notes in the back of my address book, but all I could think about was getting out of there and burying my nest egg under the dogwood tree in the backyard. Toward the end of his talk, Jack said the smartest thing I could do was invest in the stock market. Suddenly he had my attention.

"Wall Street?" I said incredulously. "You want me to play the market?"

"Absolutely," said Jack. "It's a good fit for your long-term goals and historically, it's the best way to make your money grow."

Well, the only thing I knew about history and the stock market was that periodically, it tends to completely fall apart just like my husband's high-strung Aunt Leitha. The comparison ends there, however. Aunt Leitha always gets better after a hot toddy and a good night's sleep, but the stock market can take years to recover. Besides, I grew up on stories of how rough it was during the Great Depression when Poppa Walter, my grandfather, lost his business and the family lived on nothing but porridge and turnips for weeks at a time. My favorite story about these dark days concerns Poppa Walter's cousin Sam who lost his life savings in the stock market crash of 1929 and then jumped out of his apartment window in despair. Imagine my surprise some ten years later when I was introduced to "Sam the Jumper" at Cousin Mindy's first wedding. It turns out that Sam had lived in a second floor apartment and had only sprained his ankle when he jumped. But the real kicker was that Sam had held on to his investments and become a very wealthy man down in Miami. So much for family wisdom.

With the help of my financial advisor, I did finally get involved with the stock market. Jack was careful to match my goals with the right kind of investments. If you want to play the market, or make any other investments, work with your financial advisor. As you'll see in this chapter, it's critically important to match your investments to your goals.

To Market to Market

Even though "Sam the Jumper" made enough from Wall Street to retire in style to Coral Gables, my grandfather's caution about investing in stocks was well-founded. Playing the market is much riskier than socking your savings into an interest bearing account. But as savvy investors know, the rewards are much greater, too. In fact, no other publicly traded investment has anywhere near the potential return of common stocks.

Since the 1920s when Cousin Sam started investing on Wall Street, common stocks have grown an average of over 9 percent a year, more than double the rate of either government or corporate bonds. What's more, the growth has been nearly three times the rate of inflation during that period. Sure, there have been a few "crashes" or "market corrections," as people like to call them now, but historically the stock market has always come back stronger than ever.

The last big market correction was in October 1987 when the Dow Jones Industrial Average dropped twenty-three percent on what came to be known as Black Monday. Since then, however, the Dow has risen an incredible 200 percent!

There's Nothing Common About Common Stock

So your favorite uncle just left you 100 shares of Amalgamated Consolidations,

Inc. Congratulations! You now have *equity* or ownership in a publicly traded company.

Even if you hold as little as one share of common stock, you are entitled to the same rights and privileges as Donald Trump might be if he owned 1,000,000 shares. You'd both get to vote for the next board of directors, and you might even team up to throw out the CEO if the stock price dipped. Best of all, you'd both make money if the value of the shares increased or if Amalgamated declared a dividend—a portion of the profit paid per share of stock. (Of course, The Donald would have a million votes to your one, and he'd ride to the stockholder's meeting in a chauffeured limo while you took a bus, but otherwise, you'd be two peas in a pod as fellow stockholders.)

On the downside, common stock comes with absolutely no guarantees. Companies fall on hard times or go out of business every day, and when they do, stockholders can lose some, or all, of their investment. But if you do your homework and invest for the long term, common stocks should

INVESTMENT TIP #8

NEITHER FISH NOR FOUL: WHY PREFERRED STOCK IS SOMETIMES PREFERRED...

Can't decide between stocks and bonds? Preferred stock is a way of investing in equities while drastically reducing the risk. Preferred stock differs from common stock in that the size of the dividend is guaranteed in advance and is paid before the dividends on common stock. Also, if the company were to go bankrupt, holders of preferred stock are first in line to get their money back. The downside is that preferred stock dividends don't grow if the company has a banner year, and because of that the price of these shares appreciates much slower than common stock.

be a significant part of your portfolio.

Are some times better than others to own

common stock? Absolutely.

Savvy investors know that the best time to hold common stock is when inflation is low, which usually means that interest rates are also low. Since other investors will be looking for better returns on their money than they can get with savings accounts, CDs or bonds, they will pour more and more money into the stock market, driving stock prices up for most companies. And as we have already seen, common stock outdistances the cost of living by a wide margin over the long term, making it a terrific hedge against future inflation.

THE STRAIGHT SKINNY ON GROWTH STOCKS—WHEN YOU CATCH A RISING STAR, MAKE SURE IT'S NOT A METEOR...

After I had been an active investor for a year or two, I had heard quite a collection of tall tales about the stock market. Usually they involved a friend of a friend or a distant relative who had become stinking rich by buying Xerox at 1, IBM at 5, Microsoft at 3, or like my Uncle Max, they bought "garbage" at 4.

Today of course these names represent solid, established companies, but when they started out, they were growth stocks. Typically, growth stocks are those issued by young companies in high technology areas that are expanding at a furious rate. Since they do business in areas of rapid change, such as software development or micro-processor development, there's a fair amount of risk involved. Sure, you might pick the next Microsoft out of the hat, but it might just as easily be the next Atari—a real here-today-gone-tomorrow story.

While generally a good bet over the long term, growth stocks are not a good investment if you're looking for regular income. They seldom declare dividends. Instead, company earnings tend to be folded back into the company to finance additional growth.

Income Stocks—Solid as a Rock and Often Just as Exciting

The other side of the proverbial coin are income stocks, the best of which are known as "blue chips." Income stocks typically represent companies that are very stable and have been around a long time. Rarely in hot industries, income stocks have tended to come from stodgy categories like gas and electric utilities, automakers, and telephone companies.

Not very sexy, I admit, but companies in "mature" or non-growth industries are quite reliable in paying dividends year after year. Since they don't need cash for expansion, they tend to accumulate excess funds which are then disbursed to their shareholders in the form of quarterly dividends.

Now, you'll never get rich holding income stocks, but they have a well-deserved reputation for being safe havens even during hard times. Consequently, when the stock market suffers downturns, well-established income stocks typically lose less of their value than other securities.

➤ INVESTMENT TIP #9

TORTOISE AND THE HARE: BLUE CHIPS VS. FAST GROWERS

Buying blue chips gives most people a nice rosy feeling. But that feeling often fades when the stock market booms and the corporate giants seem to be standing still. The fact is that big outfits like Ford, Coca-Cola, and General Electric don't tend to have big changes in their stock prices, which is why many of them offer regular dividends to their investors. But on the other hand, when things get tough in the financial world, those dull, solid and slow blue chips are the first place investors turn for a safe haven.

So, if regular income from your investments is one of your goals, then look into income stocks that have a long record of not only paying dividends, but of raising them as well.

The Timeless Appeal of Bonds

GETTING DOWN TO BASICS

Confused about bonds? No wonder. There are a bewildering variety of bonds on the market these days including T-bonds, T-bills, corporate bonds, zero-coupons, municipals, and agency bonds. But all you really need to know about them initially is that they are all just loans you make to the company or governmental body issuing them. Bonds are sold at a discount off their face value, and during the months or years before maturity, they will fluctuate in resale value depending on the prevailing interest rates. But when the bond reaches its maturity—the date when the agency or company has promised to redeem it—you will receive the full face value of the bond.

The longer you loan the issuing company or government agency the money, the more interest they'll pay you on your initial investment. You can buy short-term bonds that mature in a year or less; intermediate bonds that mature in two to ten years; and long bonds which can take up to thirty years to reach maturity. The long bond pays the highest rate of interest because it ties up your money for the longest period of time.

Because of this income-producing feature and the security most bonds offer, Americans have actually invested more money in bonds than in common stock. Over the last couple of decades the market for bonds has been particularly brisk because of fluctuating interest rates. You've heard the old saying, "buy low, sell high." Well, when it comes to bonds, sometimes the opposite advice is best. If you buy long-term government bonds when interest rates are high, you can sell them in the marketplace for a nice profit when interest rates are low.

Bonds are great income producers and in most cases very secure investments, but savvy investors do not usually use them as a way to accumulate assets because the

 INVESTMENT TIP #10

THE STRAIGHT SKINNY ON ZERO-COUPON BONDS

Looking for a bargain in the bond market? Then zero-coupon bonds might be for you, especially if you're not looking for short-term income. You see, zero-coupon bonds differ from regular bonds in that they sell at very deep discounts and pay out no interest (coupons) before the maturation date of the bond. The interest is allowed to build up and then is paid out in a lump sum when the bond matures.

rates of interest do not compare favorably with riskier investments such as stocks.

The Downside of Bonds

Savvy investors know that there's no such thing as a totally safe investment and that includes bonds. Okay, it's extremely rare that a corporation or a governmental body defaults on its bond payments, but it does happen. Look what happened a few years ago in Orange County, California. Orange County defaulted on their municipal bonds because they supported them by making some very risky investments that didn't work out.

Defaults aren't the only way to lose money on bonds. If you happen to buy long-term bonds with relatively low interest rates, say six to seven percent, and then the economy goes into a period of higher interest rates, you will be losing money. When the bonds reach maturity, you'll still receive their face value, but you will have forgone the higher interest you could have gotten while your money was tied up.

About the only way out is to sell the bonds before they reach maturity. You will have to sell at a loss, but you will be able to limit your losses by reinvesting your capital at a higher interest rate.

Mutual Funds: The Best of All Possible Worlds?

Whether you're a small investor with only

 INVESTMENT TIP #11

WHY IT MATTERS IF YOUR BONDS ARE CALLABLE

Amateur investors often don't realize that many corporate bonds are callable, meaning that the company that issued them can force you to redeem them before maturity if interest rates swing in their favor. So if you're buying bonds in order to profit from a future drop in interest rates, buy Long-Term Treasury Bonds which can't be called until five years before they mature.

a few hundred dollars to spare or you've got money to burn, it's hard to beat the opportunities available in today's mutual funds. What makes them so attractive to people of all classes is the fact that your investment is managed by top-of-the-line money managers at a fraction of the cost of doing it yourself.

How can they do it? Volume and highly focused investment philosophies are two of the biggest factors. Mutual funds typically pool the investments of thousands of individuals like yourself who have similar financial goals and philosophies. This creates a pool, often totaling hundreds of millions of dollars. When the fund manager goes to invest this money, he is able to get substantial discounts on fees—eighty to ninety percent over what his shareholders might pay as individuals.

No matter what your goals, there is probably a fund that fits you to a T.

You can buy funds whose focus is growth, income, growth and income (also known as balanced funds), performance (another word for high risk), conservative

INVESTMENT TIP #12

ANOTHER REASON TO BUY MUTUAL FUNDS

Experts have calculated that no-load mutual funds cost one-half to one-third as much in fees as buying and selling individual securities. When you deal in individual stocks and bonds you are charged transaction fees and commissions on both the purchase and sale of your securities, but with a no-load (no commission) mutual fund, your only cost is the annual management fee the fund charges you.

balance, international, investment grade bonds, U.S. government bonds, junk (high-risk corporate bonds), and municipal bonds—to name but a few. For the average investor, however, it's easier to think of three basic types of mutual funds: stock funds, bond funds, and money market funds.

Stock funds, obviously, invest in stocks, and aim to grow your assets over the long haul without worrying too much about short-term market gyrations. Bond funds are more conservative—meaning safer—because they put your money in bonds, which are less affected by market volatility.

 INVESTMENT TIP #13

SWITCHING FUNDS WITHOUT PAIN

Many of today's customer-oriented mutual fund companies allow their customers to switch their investments from one fund to another without fees or hassles. Suppose you have your money tied up in a growth fund that specializes in relatively high-risk technology stocks and the market suddenly turns sour. If you're with the right fund company, you could switch your funds into a capital preservation fund that invests heavily in high-rated bonds.

Money market funds are even more conservative since they put your money in short-term money instruments, such as treasury notes to insure that your basic investment will not drop in value.

You can buy mutual funds in several different ways as well. You can buy "load" funds from brokers and financial planners. Typically these carry a commission rate—called a load—of around eight percent. You can also buy no-load (meaning commission-free) funds directly from the mutual fund company. In all cases, you will be charged an annual management fee of up to one percent of the value of your investment. However, when you go to sell your no-load fund, you will pay no redemption or exit fee to get your money out—another advantage over owning individual shares of equities.

Savvy investors know that it's very difficult to beat professional money managers over the long haul. The men and women who manage mutual funds work at it full-time and have information resources you could never afford. So unless you really enjoy the process of investing in individual stocks and bonds, buying mutual funds might be the best single investment choice you could make.

Other Types of Investments

PRECIOUS METALS

For me, bullion is something my mother adds to matzo ball soup for flavor; it's not an investment. Yet millions of people around the globe have bet heavily on the value of gold, silver, and other precious metals.

You might remember how people were making a fortune speculating on gold back in the 80s. It's worth noting that inflation was king back then and people were looking for any place to park their hard-earned cash. Since inflation has been brought under control, however, gold has been anything but a sterling investment. While the stock market has been setting new highs, precious metals have been pretty much the same price they were a few years back.

So, why would you invest in precious metals? Historically, investors have flocked to gold and silver during times of uncertainty, when inflation was high and people were afraid currency would lose its value. That's when gold, in particular, tends to appreciate.

You can own gold in several different ways. You can purchase bullion units such as gold bars or ingots or you can buy coins such as Krugerrands. Personally owning gold has several drawbacks, including the safekeeping, insurance, and moving it when you want to sell. Instead of actually possessing the gold, you can buy gold certificates. Issued by banks, brokers and dealers in precious metals, these are basically warehouse receipts that give you ownership without the headache of possession. They are much more easily redeemed than bullion.

By far the easiest way of investing in

precious metals, however, is to either buy shares in a mining or refining company, or to purchase shares in a mutual fund that invests in mining companies. This way you can profit when the price of precious metals appreciates and/or when companies do well.

LAND, HO!

My father-in-law, the frugal Reverend Smith, took my husband aside when we were first married and gave him the following good advice: "Buy real estate, son. God isn't making any more of it." Unfortunately, however, he didn't tell us *when* to buy it.

Even though land has been historically a good way to grow your net worth, it's still not foolproof. If you pay too much for anything—including real estate—you will definitely lose money. I know because we bought our little castle right at the height of land fever in New York. Back in 1987, you couldn't buy a doghouse for under $100,000, and if you wanted a couple of modest bedrooms and a bath, you were staring $200,000 right in the face.

Nine years and a few massive layoffs later, Richard, the boys, and I are still happily ensconced in suburbia, along with our giant mortgage and a house worth 85 percent of what it cost. We've paid off some of the principal over the years, but if we had to sell tomorrow, the sad fact is that we'd take a loss.

Our story aside, investing in real estate, especially home ownership, remains one of the best ways for the average person to build a nest egg for the future. Real estate tends to grow in value during inflationary times, and the interest you pay on mortgage loans for your home or rental property is tax deductible.

Apart from home ownership, you can also invest in undeveloped land, commercial properties, condos, cooperatives, and rental houses. If being a landlord is attractive to you, take a long look at the drawbacks first. You'll have to deal with property taxes; fire, flood, and liability insurance; and the potential loss of the investment's value through changes in demographics, the local economy, or because of changes in government policies.

REIT: A New Way to Invest in Real Estate

REIT stands for Real Estate Investment Trust, and it's a way for the small investor to share in the potential profits and tax benefits of large real estate development deals. In many respects REITs are like mutual funds. Both attract money from a large number of private and institutional investors and then invest the funds in a diverse group of projects or, in some cases, mortgages related to development projects. It's not unusual for a single REIT to be involved in developing shopping malls, apartment complexes, industrial parks, and resorts in many parts of the country. Consequently, the individual investor not only avoids the hassles associated with managing property, but enjoys the benefits of diversification.

REITs are also a good inflation hedge since real estate traditionally goes up in value as inflation increases. And over the last five years, some major REITs have enjoyed double-digit returns. However, REITs are not without risk. Shares of REITs are traded like stocks or mutual funds and can go up and down in price depending on market conditions.

THE REAL STORY ON LIFE INSURANCE

The first time someone tried to sell me life insurance was back in college. A Young Republican type who couldn't have been more than a year or two out of school himself came by my dorm and tried to sell me a "starter" policy. He showed me a book full of clippings about kids my own age who had died due to car accidents, exotic diseases, or downed power lines. Overcome with romantic thoughts of my own mortality, I was all set to sign on the dotted line for a "no premiums until you graduate" deal when my roommate arrived and broke the spell. And a good thing, too, because it was a terrible deal!

The fact is, the agent was trying to sell me *whole* or *cash value* life insurance. Whole life insurance not only gives you insurance, it *matures*: After a given period of time, it repays you the money you've invested, plus a modest return. Sounds good, doesn't it? There's another kind of life insurance, too, called *term* life, which is more like auto insurance. You pay a flat rate, and only get your money back by meeting the terms of the policy—in this case, by dying. Doesn't sound so good, does it?

The plain fact is that whole life insurance is one of the worst investments you can make. Experts will tell you that as an investment life insurance makes sense for a very small percentage of the population, most of whom are already independently wealthy!

Whole life insurance is a waste of your hard-earned money. For equal amounts of coverage, term life insurance will cost you approximately one-eighth the premiums of whole life insurance! So, if you're considering life insurance (and you ought to be), buy term. And if you're concerned about putting away money for your retirement (and you ought to be), put the money you save into your IRA or a 401K plan at work.

Here's something else to think about. When you buy whole or cash value life insurance, somewhere between 50 and 100 percent of your first year's premium is used to pay the salesman's commission, which means that it must be a much better deal for the insurance company than for you.

MORE ALPHABET SOUP: IRAS, SEPS, KEOGH, AND 401KS

Savvy investors know that when someone offers you a good deal, you should take it. Whether you're self-employed, like my husband, Richard, or toil away at a giant corporation, there's no better deal around than a retirement account. Retirement accounts are especially great if your employer matches your contributions in any way. Many employers will match you 50 cents on the dollar; some will go even higher up to a certain threshold.

Now for a few quick definitions. IRA stands for Individual Retirement Account, and anyone can set one up at a bank or brokerage house. A 401K is a retirement account that requires employee contributions, but is often matched by the employer. A KEOGH is a plan for self-employed people that allows them to invest up to 20 percent of their annual income tax free until retirement. SEP stands for simplified employee pension plan and is much like a KEOGH plan but with less paperwork.

All of these plans have a couple of things in common. They're salary reduction plans which lower your taxable income, allowing you to sock away a portion of your paycheck in a retirement account. Also, your money is allowed to compound without taxation until you begin withdrawing it at age fifty-nine and a half.

However, if you should need money before that age, you will be subject to a ten percent penalty upon withdrawal—one of the few drawbacks to retirement accounts.

Canada's Registered Retirement Savings Plans

In many ways, Canada's Registered Retirement Savings Plans (RRSPs) are identical to American IRAs. They allow you to put aside a portion of your earned income each year into a designated retirement account, thereby lowering your tax liability for the year while saving for the future. Also, RRSPs allow the value of your account to grow without tax liability until such time as you retire, at which time it is taxed as ordinary income. Furthermore, like IRAs, RRSPs can contain a wide variety of financial instruments, including individual stocks, all manner of mutual funds, corporate bonds, and even Canadian savings bonds. However, there are some important differences which make RRSPs superior to American IRAs.

For instance, whereas IRAs impose a stiff penalty for withdrawal of funds from the account before age fifty-nine and a half, regardless of the circumstances, RRSPs allow the investor to withdraw funds at any time without penalty. The investor must, however, pay ordinary income taxes on the amount withdrawn. This important feature allows the savvy investor to use RRSPs in several ways not open to their American cousins and their IRAs. Here are several of the possibilities:

- Tax-averaging — Every family has periods when income drops or rises dramatically due to situations such as illness, a return to school, a new baby, sudden job loss, or on the bright side, an unusually large bonus or the return to work by a family member. Canadians have the ability to average out the tax implications of these dips and rises by contributing heavily to their RRSPs during good years to reduce their tax rates, and then during lean years, they can make withdrawals without penalty, thereby *collapsing* their RRSPs.

- Income Splitting — As long as your total contributions don't exceed the statutory limit, you can make contributions to your spouse's RRSP as well as your own. The advantage to this strategy is that once you and your spouse begin withdrawals at retirement, the amounts will be taxed separately and collectively at lower rates. Another positive aspect of this strategy is the fact that Old Age Security benefits will be less likely to be reduced due to levels of income from your RRSPs.

- The Pension Income Tax Credit — If you rollover your RRSP into an annuity or Registered Retirement Income Fund (RRIF), your RRSP funds qualify as retirement income, thereby exempting the first $1,000 paid to you each year from taxes. If you've taken advantage of the income splitting strategy, both you and your spouse can qualify for the pension income tax credit, thereby sheltering $2,000 a year.

With growing questions about the future viability of government pension plans on both sides of the border, individual plans such as RRSPs are more important than ever before. Even though the Canadian government has taken steps in the last couple of years to limit contributions to RRSPs, they are still far and away the best option Canadians have to reduce their tax burden while preparing a nest egg for the future.

COLLECTIBLES— WHY BEAUTY IS IN THE EYE OF THE BEHOLDER

My Aunt Anita from Brooklyn collects decorative sugar spoons and ceramic figurines, mostly songbirds and cherubs. Every nook and cranny of her apartment is full of the stuff. My husband, Richard, has every Superman comic he ever bought, plus twenty years of baseball cards in a steamer trunk in our attic. He's convinced that someday they'll be worth enough to send the kids off to medical school. I'm not so sure.

The idea behind collectibles as an investment is that whatever you're collecting is relatively rare and will become more valuable over time because of its rarity and desirability to other collectors.

Savvy investors know that collectibles, whether they're van Goghs, diamond tiaras, or matchbooks are problematic as investments. Recent studies have shown that even world-class art cannot always be counted on to do much more than keep pace with inflation, especially once you factor in the cost of insurance and restorations. Experts will tell you that if you must collect, do so because you love it, not for speculative reasons. And whatever you do, don't call Richard if you've got baseball cards to sell!

CHAPTER FOUR

Why You Should Invest In Certain Products

INVESTMENT STRATEGIES

My husband, Richard, has a friend named Doug who lives down the block. As far as I can tell, Richard and Doug have nothing in common but an inexplicable love for golf. Don't get me wrong. I love manicured fairways and flowers, but watching golf on TV is like getting a guided tour of Forest Lawn Cemetery. Still, every time there's a big tournament on, Richard and Doug retire to our den where they sit in twin recliners looking like two pudgy astronauts about to be blasted into space. When they're not eating, they fill the air with golf clichés as the lack of action unfolds on the giant television screen: pearls of wisdom such as, "Must've pulled it" and "Came over that one" and "Never up, never in."

I can't make heads or tails of most of it, but there's one saying that speaks to me as an investor: "It's not how; it's how many." When I first heard it, I asked Richard what it meant, he looked at me blankly and said, "There are no style points in golf." Great help. Fortunately, Doug was just returning from the kitchen with a plate of steaming nachos, and the few minutes away from golf was reviving some of his brain cells. He explained that the expression meant it doesn't matter how you do it, or how pretty your stroke is, it's the final score that counts.

The same is definitely true when it comes to investing for the future. There are a million strategies and techniques that investors swear by, and presumably they've all worked well for someone at some point, or they wouldn't still be around. Some are very technical. Others are as simple as throwing darts at the financial page—a technique that's been known to beat the experts from time to time, although I wouldn't recommend it over the long haul. The trick is to find an approach that will be successful for you and your unique situation.

So, in this section we'll be looking at strategies that savvy investors use in particular times and situations to get a better-than-average return on their investments. Remember, just like in golf, there are no style points in investing!

BUY AND HOLD

Year in and year out, Warren Buffett of Des Moines, Iowa, is near the top of the list of the world's wealthiest men. As CEO of the investment firm and holding company named Berkshire Hathaway, Buffett is the antithesis of the frantic Wall Street trader. You've seen them in the movies, with a phone in each ear, yelling, "buy" at the top of their lungs into one phone and "sell" into the other. Buffett has made billions of dollars for himself and others by quietly buying stocks he really believes in and then holding onto them for as long as possible. This is what's known as the "buy and hold" strategy.

Of course, in order to play the game the way Buffett does, you've got to do your homework, searching out companies with good financial stories and a leadership posture in their industries. Once you have located companies with that kind of value, you make your investments and then watch the stock prices rise while the companies prosper. In the meantime, you avoid all the commissions and capital-gains taxes you might have paid over the years by heavy trading, which helps your assets grow that much faster.

Sounds simple, doesn't it? Well, it is in concept, but the trick is in locating the right companies to invest in, and then having the patience to wait for them to increase in value. While you wait, you've also got to turn a blind eye to the stock market's ups and downs and keep your attention focused firmly on the companies you've picked. Clearly, not everyone has the patience or the time to use this strategy, but it's hard to argue with Buffett's success.

A QUICK P/E (FISCAL EDUCATION) CLASS

One of the time-honored tools for investors like Buffett is the price/earnings ratio, also known as the P/E multiple, or simply, *the multiple*. Basically, the P/E ratio is an equation used for describing the value of a stock. You get it by dividing the price of the stock by the company's profits. For example, if McDonalds is selling for $100 per share, and is earning $10 per share, it would have a P/E ratio of 10. This would tell the smart investor two things: that Arch Deluxes and Big Macs were really moving; and that the stock was selling for 10 times the earnings of the previous year.

If you think all this is too complicated, don't worry. Someone else has done the work for you. To find the multiple of a stock that you're interested in, go to the financial section of your morning paper and look up the stock. You'll find the P/E multiple listed along with the price.

How do you know a good P/E ratio from a bad one? Here's a simple rule of thumb: the lower the P/E ratio, the better. Any number below 15 is good and numbers below 10 are considered outstanding. The reason experts like low numbers is that you can use the P/E ratio to determine how long it will take to earn back your investment. In the case of McDonalds, it would take 10 years.

MORE ABOUT P/E (ADVANCED)

Now that you're all excited about having a simple system for buying stocks, it's only fair that I tell you why it's not foolproof.

Number One: P/E multiples can be high not because the companies are bad stocks to own, but simply because the market in general has been *bidded up*. At the time I'm writing this, Wall Street has been enjoying the biggest bull market in history with the Dow Jones Industrial Averages soaring past 5,500. Because so many people want so much stock, it's inevitable that stock prices will rise faster than earnings. As a result, some very profitable companies are overpriced. Their P/E ratio climbs. In short, they are question-able buys.

Number Two: P/E multiples can be high because the company is a new outfit in a growth industry. Such companies are so busy growing that their earnings haven't really kicked in yet. Investors who are looking for the next Microsoft or Xerox will buy stocks with high multiples if they have good reason to believe the stock is going to take off.

Number Three: a low P/E can mean that the company is an older, established com-pany with few growth prospects. While you can usually rely on such companies for regular dividends and some measure of security, don't expect their stock prices to rise significantly.

By dividing a stock's current price by com-pany's earnings per share, you'll get the stock's price/earnings ratio or multiple. As you've already learned, this number also equals the number of years it will take you to earn back your initial investment at the stock's current value.

BUY WHAT'S RIGHT
UNDER YOUR NOSE

Peter Lynch, the former head of Fidelity's Magellan Fund, argues strongly that the average person knows a great deal more about the market than the so-called experts. His argument is that it takes a long time for Wall Street to analyze young growing companies, and to put them on their *buy* lists. But the average person already knows about these companies, because he or she is using their products and services every day. In a way, we're all experts on something, whether it's the kind of software we use or the best place to get our oil changed at a fair price. The trick is to recognize what we already know and then act upon it!

Let me give you a personal example. My husband, Richard, was raised in Georgia and Florida and is quite a connoisseur of iced tea, known in some circles as *the house wine of the South.* When we first settled in Long Island, Richard discovered a bottled iced tea that he absolutely adored and started buying it by the case. It turned out that it was made by a couple of guys who lived in the next town over. If you haven't guessed already, the name of the company was Snapple.

I wish I could tell you that we rushed right out and bought the stock, but we didn't. It was two years before we took "the iced tea plunge," by which time the stock had climbed quite a bit. We still made a very nice profit on Snapple when they sold out to Quaker Oats, but it was nothing like it could have been if I could only have seen what was right under Richard's nose!

MORE COMMONSENSE ADVICE

Now the fact that Richard loved Snapple would not have been a good reason to buy the stock. There are plenty of wonderful products out there owned by companies that are badly managed, deeply in debt, overly diversified or have a host of other drawbacks.

If you've got a wonderful new product or service you'd like to invest in, do some research on the company. This is a good project to ask your financial advisor to help you with. Among other things, you need to find out the following:

1. What percentage of total sales does the new product or service represent?

If the new product comes from a large company such as Bristol Myers, then chances are it will have little impact on the value of the stock.

2. What about the company's management?

Ford Motor Company wouldn't be one of the Big Three Automakers if Henry and his crew hadn't been pretty shrewd. Do the managers of the company you're looking at have the right stuff to take their company to the top?

3. How much debt is the company carrying?

If they have too much debt, it might be hard for them to reach profitability, no matter how good their products are.

ONE-STOP SHOPPING: THE VALUE LINE APPROACH

Now that I've introduced the issue of research, it's time to talk more about The Value Line Investment Surveys. Value Line is quite possibly the single most valuable source of information on publicly traded companies there is. So much so, that some investors have made it a system unto itself.

Available through stockbrokers and libraries or by subscription, Value Line Investment Surveys provide the individual investor with a wealth of easily accessible information on top companies. The surveys include P/E ratios; rankings on the company's safety as an investment, expected performance over the next year; company profile; earnings per share; and tables and charts on historical performance.

Value Line doesn't follow every stock, but they do cover 1700—quite a considerable number. The stocks are ranked in five groups according to their value. There are 100 stocks in the first group; 300 in the second group; 900 in the third; 300 in the fourth, and 100 in the fifth and last group.

So what's the system? Well, investors who limited their purchases to group one stocks over the years have made an extraordinary amount of money. The system is different from buy and sell, however. Each time a stock drops from group one into group two or lower, you must sell the stock and buy additional group one stocks to fill out your holdings.

The system is based on two premises: First, it's always smart to buy stocks with good fundamental performance. Second, when companies are on a roll, sheer momentum tends to keep their stock going up for a while. When their momentum drops off or their fundamentals change, it's time to get a new horse.

DOES ANYBODY KNOW WHAT TIME IT IS?

We've talked a lot about choosing investments based on their inherent value, but there is another school of thinkers more concerned with the market as a whole. These brave folks are known as market timers.

Market timers realize that you have to strike while the iron is hot: that is, invest when the market is headed up. If you are successful in catching the wave of the market—whether you're investing in stocks, bonds, real estate, or even gold—the individual investments you make are of secondary importance.

How do market timers know when to buy and when to sell? Typically, they follow data such as interest rates, the Consumer Price Index, the Dow Jones Industrial Averages, and unemployment figures. When interest rates are reaching their peaks and inflation is rising, market timers might shift their holdings from stocks to bonds, locking in good returns. The market timer does this with the expectation that the high interest rates will make CDs and bonds more attractive and that investors will switch to them from stocks, causing stock prices to plummet. Then, when inflation is brought under control and interest rates drop, market timers begin placing their money back into stocks and start the cycle all over again.

While there are many things that can be learned from market timers, it's not a good approach for the average investor. The time involved is enormous and the risk is huge that at any particular time you could be wrong about the movement of financial markets. The danger is that by the time you realize the market is trending up or down, it may already be too late to do anything constructive about it.

DIVERSIFICATION, OR THE WISDOM OF PUTTING ALL YOUR EGGS IN SEVERAL BASKETS

Of all investment strategies, diversification seems like the most logical and prudent to pursue. Simply put, diversification means

INVESTMENT TIP #14

What To Do When the Market is Soaring, and Everything Costs Too Much

The world's richest investor, Warren Buffett, has had to confront this situation a number of times in his career, and his approach is a good lesson for us all. His solution? At one point, Buffett actually got out of the stock market entirely, moving everything into cash and returning his investors' funds to them until the market, and prices, settled down.

spreading the risk of loss around by placing your assets in different categories of investments. Typically, a diversified portfolio includes stocks in different industries, or in non-related categories like stocks, bonds, and precious metals. If you're properly diversified, when market conditions change you won't be hurt. At least one of your investment categories is bound to go up in value, balancing out any losses you might suffer in another category.

Historically, diversification seems to make sense. It seems as if each decade is good for at least one type of investment and not so good for another. For instance, during the 1970s when inflation was high, precious metals soared, while stocks and bonds dipped in value.

The only danger in diversification is that when you spread your risks across several kinds of investments, you also reduce your potential return. This is particularly problematic during a major bull market. Savvy investors know that strong markets are your best chance to make substantial gains and are wary of dampening their returns by focusing too much on diversification.

DOLLAR COST AVERAGING

Dollar Cost Averaging is an investment approach that's one part discipline and two parts bargain hunting. If you carefully clip and save coupons to hold down the family

DOLLAR COST AVERAGING

Regular Investment	Purchased Stock Price	Shares Purchased
$200	$20	10
$200	$40	5
$200	$50	4
$200	$40	5
$200	$100	2
$200	$100	2

Average Value Per Share = $58.33

Average Cost Per Share = $42.85

grocery bill, you might have just the temperament to try it.

Also known as the *constant dollar plan*, this system requires that you make regular investments of a set amount in a chosen investment vehicle. The investment could be an individual stock or group of stocks, or it might be mutual funds. Since the price of your investment choice will vary over time, you'll get fewer shares for your money when the price is high. On the other hand, when the price is low, you'll pay less per share and get more shares. You benefit because buying more shares when prices are low lowers the average cost of your purchases.

Dollar Cost Averaging has the added benefit of letting you take your eye off the market. As long as you're buying at regular intervals, you can be sure you're getting the best price on your securities, regardless of whether the market is up or down. *Dollar Cost Averaging* is most effective when applied to long-term equity investments such as common stocks and mutual funds.

STAGGERED BOND MATURITIES

When you're investing in bonds, you've got to make sure you're getting the maximum return possible as well as limiting your risk of loss. A technique called staggering maturities or portfolio laddering is a system that some investors have had very good luck with in the past.

Here's how it works: You begin the process by buying equal amounts of bonds with different maturity dates. For this example, we'll use securities with maturations of one, three, and five years. When the one-year security matures, you use the money to buy another quantity of five-year bonds. Two years later, when the three-year bonds mature, you buy more five-year bonds, and so on. Eventually, you'd have all your money in five-year bonds, with a batch maturing every two years.

There are several benefits to staggering maturities, including keeping the maturities in your portfolio on a regular cycle. Since you will be redeeming bonds at regular intervals, you will remain relatively liquid

INVESTMENT TIP #15

WHAT TO DO IF YOU'VE GOT VERY LITTLE TO INVEST

Even if you've got as little as $50 to invest, there's a mutual fund out there that will help you get started investing in equities. Normally, very small investors are boxed out of the stock market because commissions and fees eat up their meager war chests. The sample funds listed on page 127, however, welcome everyone. Ask your financial advisor about the funds that best suit your needs.

and have the opportunity to get the best possible yields during any given cycle. If interest rates drop, you will be protected because the bonds you hold with higher interest rates will rise in value. If interest rates rise, you will capture the benefit through your short-term investments.

INVESTMENT TIP #16

A DIVIDEND BY ANY
OTHER NAME...

If you're investing in the long-term, large dividends are not always such a wonderful thing. Rather than paying dividends, aggressive companies plow excess profits back into the company to finance future growth and earnings.

Sometimes paying big dividends is just the sign of a prosperous company in a mature industry with no prospects of growth. At other times, however, it merely shows a lack of imagination on the part of top management.

REINVESTING DIVIDENDS

If you're a cautious investor who favors blue-chip stocks because of the dividends they pay, here's a cost-effective way to increase your assets. Most dividends do not represent a large amount of money—typically only a

MUTUAL FUNDS FOR
SMALL INVESTORS

Fund Name	Minimum Initial Investment	Maximum Subsequent Investment
M.S.B. Fund	$50	$25
Portico Int Bond-Retail	$100	$100
Portico Tax-Exempt Int-Retail	$100	$100
Dupree KY Tax-Free Income	$100	$100
Capstone Gov't Income	$200	$0
National Industries	$250	$25
AARP Balanced Stock & Bond	$500	$0
Sentry	$500	$50
Fidelity Retirement Growth	$500	$250

few dollars a share. You can make those dividends work extra hard for you, however, by reinvesting them in the same stocks.

Most companies have well-organized dividend reinvestment programs, and some of them will absorb the commissions you would normally pay to buy the additional stock. What's more, many companies will also sell you the additional stock at a discount. So at the end of the day, you've actually compounded the value of your dividends by reinvesting them, and you've increased the size of your portfolio without laying out any additional cash.

SOMETIMES IT'S GOOD TO BE CONTRARY....

Like a lot of people's mothers, my mom is a natural born contrarian—at least with me, her only daughter. If I say white, she says black. If I make turkey dressing outside the bird, she says it's got to be stuffed inside the bird. Got the picture? I know she only does it because she still worries about me after all these years, but sometimes I wish she'd channel all that negative energy into the stock market where it would do her some good!

You see, there's a whole class of investors called contrarians who have made a bundle doing the opposite of what everybody else is doing. Their position is that if everybody believes the market is going one way, it's bound to go the other way. And they're not just being negative when they say that. Contrarians argue that so-called stock market experts tend to predict the market is going up when they personally have sunk all of their capital into it, and conversely, the same people will predict a market downturn when they've already sold their holdings. In the contrarian philosophy, the very actions of the market predictors help influence events in the opposite direction.

Since the contrarian does the opposite of what the mass of investors is doing, he buys when everyone else is selling. He thereby picks up securities at a discount, and then sits back to watch the price rise when the market heats up again. To follow this strategy you don't even have to be a market watcher. There are a number of mutual funds that invest according to contrarian strategy. Naturally, the only downside to being a contrarian is when you're wrong. For instance, take the bull market of the early nineties. If you took a contrarian position after the first year or so, you would have missed one of the biggest bull markets in history.

GO GLOBAL!

Savvy investors go where the action is. Increasingly the hottest markets are outside of North America. Markets such as Hong Kong, Ireland, France, Austria, and the Netherlands have actually outperformed Wall Street over the last ten years. If investing outside the country makes you feel squeamish, look at it this way: Global investing is nothing more than a good diversification strategy to make sure that you're not missing out on growth opportunities elsewhere when our economy slows down.

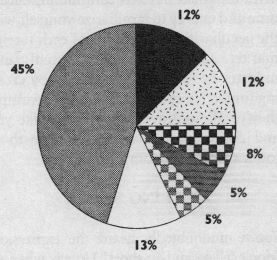

An Example of a Balanced Portfolio

12%

12%

45%

8%

5%

5%

13%

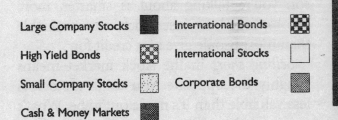

■ Large Company Stocks	▦ International Bonds
▨ High Yield Bonds	☐ International Stocks
⣿ Small Company Stocks	▒ Corporate Bonds
■ Cash & Money Markets	

Obviously, to be a successful overseas investor, you'd have to commit significant time and energy to familiarize yourself with the peculiarities and politics of each foreign market. Once again, the mutual fund industry has come to the rescue. By creating funds that specialize in global investing, they've allowed average investors like you and me to participate in the growth of today's world economy.

SELLING SHORT

You've undoubtedly heard the expression, "don't sell so-and-so short." Usually when we say something like that, it means that the person you're talking about is smarter, more accomplished, or just much more valuable than most people give him credit for.

Selling short in the stock market means roughly the opposite: you think a stock is less valuable than it's made out to be. What's more, you're willing to bet that its asking price will soon drop.

Fascinating, you say, but how do you make money being so negative?

First, you borrow the stock you think is overvalued from your friendly full-service broker. It's the broker's job to find you the stock, and he gives it to you with the understanding that you will replace it, regardless of the cost. Next, you sell this stock you've borrowed at its present higher price. When the stock falls in value as you predicted, you buy it at the lower price and give it back to the broker you borrowed it from in the first place. And best of all, you pocket the difference—minus commissions of course.

Shorting stocks is not for the faint-hearted, however. If you guess wrong on the direction of the market, you will have to replace the stocks you borrowed at the higher price, thereby losing money, plus commissions!

ASSET ALLOCATION

My husband, Richard, is a lovely man, but due to a genetic tendency toward big shoulders and too much weight lifting as a teenager, you can't find a suit off the rack to fit him. If the chest and shoulders are just right, the sleeves are five inches too long and the pants have to be taken in so much that the back pockets touch. After suffering through years of uncomfortable, badly fitting suits, Richard finally found a solution: a custom tailor from Hong Kong who comes to the city once a year. The prices are reasonable, Richard gets a suit that fits him like a glove, and I go along to pick out the fabric. So everybody's happy.

What does this little story have to do with investing? If you want something that really fits your needs—whether it's a new suit or an investment plan, you've got to have it tailor-made. Asset allocation is the name of the strategy that tries to fit your objectives, financial profile, and comfort level with risk, to an investment plan.

For example: Let's say you are a young working mother with two small children. Your goals are to build up a college fund for them and to prepare for your own retirement. With time on your side, you might invest heavily in stocks, since they will give you higher returns over the long haul, even though they might be riskier short-term.

On the other hand, if you are only ten years away from retirement, you might lean heavily toward safe, income-generating instruments such as government bonds and blue-chip stocks. Then there are those of you whose needs fall into the middle range, requiring a balance of stocks, bonds, and liquid investments such as money market funds. If you are confused as to how to allocate your investment money, review the goals you developed in the first section. Then, talk it over with your financial advisor.

MOMENTUM INVESTING

Everybody loves a winner, especially in the stock market. That's why when a stock is suddenly discovered by the market, it continues to go up in price for quite some time—especially if its fundamentals are sound. Investors who take advantage of this psychology are called *momentum investors*.

A great many managers of successful mutual funds tend to use this philosophy, buying stocks when they first begin their climb up the ladder. Of course, the very fact that a large fund has bought a significant amount of any stock is usually enough to drive the price up. This makes the stock attractive to both individual investors and institutions. When they begin to buy, it drives the stock up even further.

However, when the momentum starts to lag, fund managers sell at a profit and move on, which can cause a previously hot stock to drop by half of its value in a day. So, if you want to play the momentum game, be careful to sell before the big guys do.

OPTIONS, WARRANTS, AND COMMODITIES

Did you know you can make money investing without having to actually buy the securities involved? By buying warrants, options, and commodities futures—investments that "bet" on the future prices of stocks, bonds, or commodities—it's possible to make large profits if you can stand the risk. Many investors buy such instruments with no intention of ever taking possession of the product. They make their money by selling them to other investors before the dates they must be exercised. Of course, you can lose your shirt—and your house—in this type of speculating, so the average investor should stay well away from these investments. And if your financial advisor suggests them, maybe it's time for a change of advisors.

Of the three, warrants are probably the safest thing for the average investor because they're relatively cheap and your risk is limited to the price of the warrant. Basically, warrants guarantee that you can buy a certain number of shares of a company's stock at a set price for a certain period of time. What's more, the cost of the warrant is typically a fraction of the cost of a share of stock. Savvy investors buy warrants when they feel that a stock's price is bound to increase well beyond the price guaranteed by the warrant. Companies issue warrants because it offers them an additional means of raising capital prior to actually issuing new stock. The investor takes the chance that the warrant will expire before the stock reaches a desirable price. In this case, the investor usually chooses not to exercise the warrant and loses the initial small investment.

Options are similar to warrants in that the investor is betting on the future price of the security. Options are different in that investors can bet either that the stock or bond will go up in value, in which case the investment is called a *call*, or that it will go down in value, in which case it's called a *put*.

Commodities are essentially bets on the future prices of raw materials such as gasoline, wheat, corn, and pork bellies. If you buy a contract for wheat at $3.00 a bushel and then there's a bumper crop of wheat that drives the price down to $2.50 a bushel, you'll take a big loss. On the other hand, if the crop is smaller than expected and prices rise, you could be a big winner.

But any way you look at it, this is a game for speculators.

CHAPTER FIVE

The
Hows of
Investing

EVERYTHING YOU NEED KNOW ABOUT THE MARKETS

Unlike most people I know, my frugal father-in-law is totally unafraid of tackling new things. In the years I've known him, he's learned how to make the most delicious marmalade from the oranges that grow in his yard; and he's become a highly skilled woodworker, restoring family heirlooms. He's mastered genealogy, too, tracing his family tree all the way back to the tenth century and in the process, establishing connections to such luminaries as George Washington and Mormon leader Joseph Smith.

When I asked him recently how he managed to learn all these new skills, he fished around in his wallet for a moment and pulled out a library card. Then he said, "If you can read, and have a little patience, you can learn how to do just about anything."

And that includes investing. A lot of what you'll need to know in order to make investment decisions is readily available in your newspaper and local library. The problem for most people is that their eyes glaze over when they turn to the financial pages. It's like picking up *Moby Dick* when you're just learning to read. Panic sets in, and a little voice in your head screams, "Where are the pictures?"

Well, after reading this section, you may not be ready to buy a seat on the stock exchange. You will, however, be able to read annual reports and *The Wall Street Journal* well enough to track your portfolio, and make some decisions about future investments, too!

WHAT YOU NEED TO KNOW ABOUT THE NEW YORK STOCK EXCHANGE

When people picture Wall Street, they see frenzied traders running around the floor of the New York Stock Exchange (NYSE). Founded in 1792, it's the oldest and biggest exchange in the United States with a membership of some 1366 *seats*.

The seats are owned by individuals instead of firms, but the owners are typically senior members of securities companies. All told, roughly 550 firms are represented.

One of the unique aspects of the NYSE is their system of specialists, members who specialize in making a market for the particular stocks and bonds that they handle. The majority of member firms trade on behalf of individual investors and institutions, but there are a few members of the exchange who do nothing but trade their own portfolios.

Most of the 1600 companies traded on the NYSE tend to be older, well-established companies that can meet the exchange's tough requirements for size and stability. Their stocks—along with bonds, warrants, and options—are traded on the floor of the exchange at twenty-two locations called trading posts.

WHAT YOU NEED TO KNOW ABOUT THE AMERICAN STOCK EXCHANGE

Until 1921, the American Stock Exchange (ASE) was officially called the "Curb Exchange"—a designation still used by industry insiders. Located in New York, the ASE focuses on small and medium-sized companies, although a number of large utilities are also traded there. Also traded at the ASE are stock options, including those of NYSE securities, over the counter stocks and a great many foreign stocks as well. The ASE is the second largest American exchange in terms of volume.

WHAT YOU NEED TO KNOW ABOUT NASDAQ

You may have seen some rather dramatic television ads that breathlessly proclaim NASDAQ to be the stock market for the twenty-first century. So what is NASDAQ and how is so different from the other financial markets?

NASDAQ stands for the National Association of Securities Dealers Automated Quotations. NASDAQ runs a computerized system that gives dealers and brokers around the country prices for stocks and bonds traded *over-the-counter* as well as for New York Stock Exchange-listed securities. NASDAQ is not a physical place like the New York Stock Exchange. It is rather a *virtual* market where transactions are conducted via telephone and computers rather than on the floor of an actual building.

NASDAQ stocks overwhelmingly represent newer and smaller companies with relatively few assets and small stock prices that cannot qualify for listing on the traditional exchanges. NASDAQ stocks are also more volatile and therefore riskier than NYSE listings. But with higher volatility comes the opportunity for greater profits attractive to so many investors.

How to Read the Business News

STOCK QUOTATIONS

52 Weeks		Stock	Sym	Div	Yld %	PE	Vol 100s	Hi	Lo	Cl	Net Chg
Hi	Lo										
73 5/8	55	UnPacific	UNP	1.72	2.4	16	15821	74	72	72	+5/8

I'll admit the first time I opened the financial pages and saw something like this, it made about as much sense to me as the periodic tables did in high school chemistry. But after my financial advisor gave me a quick fifteen minute tutorial, everything began to clear up. Let's take the items category by category:

Hi Lo — These numbers represent the highest and lowest prices of the stock for the past year. Savvy investors look to them for an indication of how "volatile" the stock is, or its potential for both profit and loss.

Stock — Here's where the company name appears, listed alphabetically and usually abbreviated. The stock name is followed by the ticker symbol.

Net Div — This figure indicates what the company is expected to pay as a yearly dividend. If no figure is listed in this area, the company doesn't pay cash dividends.

Yld % — This figure, which is read *percent yield*, tells you how much of a dividend you get in relation to stock price. If you divide the dividend by the closing price of the stock, you can calculate this figure for yourself.

PE — The P/E ratio or *multiple* expresses the relationship between the company's earnings and its stock price. The P/E ratio is calculated by dividing the stock's closing price by the company's earnings per share. Because it's related to company earnings, as well as the company's *value*, professional investors watch this number closely.

Vol — Multiply this number by 100, and you'll know how many shares of this stock traded the day before. This is important because it expresses the market's level of interest in the company.

Net Chg — This number is a comparison of the stock's closing price with its price the day before. If it's preceded by a minus, it means the price is lower than yesterday's. If it's accompanied by a plus, it means the closing price is higher.

Hi Lo Close — These figures at the far right of the listing show you the previous day's highest, lowest, and closing price for the stock in question.

Note: If the letters pf or pr follow the company's name, it means that the stock is preferred stock, rather than common stock. If the letters wt follow the company name, then the listing is for warrants rather than common stock.

TALE OF THE TAPES

If you've got cable television, and who doesn't these days, you've undoubtedly seen the stock market quotations running underneath the talking heads on some cable news channels. Electronic quotations like these have replaced the old paper *ticker tapes* of years past that connected investors with the stock exchanges. While ticker tape parades on Wall Street may have suffered from the switch to plain confetti, small investors around the country have reason to rejoice: they now have more access to more information than ever before. Here's a quick lesson that will enable you to read ticker tapes with the best of them.

Most electronic ticker tapes display two different bands. The top band is typically a consolidation of reports from the New York Stock Exchange, the American Stock Exchange and some regional markets,

INVESTMENT TIP #17

POINTS & FRACTIONS

When you hear that your favorite technology stock just closed down 2 points or shot up 3-1/8, do you know what that means in terms of dollars and cents? Actually, it's pretty easy. When you're talking about stock prices, a point is a dollar and everything less than a point is expressed in fractions of a dollar. To illustrate: 6-1/2 equals $6.50; 6-1/4 equals $6.25; and 6-1/8 is equal to $6.13.

while the bottom band is dedicated to NASDAQ over-the-counter stocks.

The first letters you see are the stock's symbols, usually an abbreviation of the company name. For instance, Dow Chemical's symbol is DOW; Bank One's is ONE; and Time Warner's is TWX. After the symbol, you'll often see other letters that indicate that the stock may be preferred (pr). It may also be a

certain class of common stock, in which case
the symbol will be followed by a period and
then a capital letter designating the class of
the issue. For example, Acme.B would mean
Acme Corporation's class B common stock.
(Stocks are broken into classes when companies offer different versions of the security.
They're usually differentiated by dividend
policies, voting rights, and price.) Other
abbreviations you should look for include
WS for warrants, and rt for rights.
Sometimes the symbol will be followed by an
ampersand and a capital letter as well. This
means that the trade in question took place
on a particular exchange. Here's a list of the
most popular exchanges: American Stock
Exchange (A); New York Stock Exchange
(N); NASDAQ (T, meaning third or other
market).

Now what about those numbers following the symbol? They indicate both the
price of the stock and the volume of shares
traded. For example, TWX 33-1/2 means
that 100 shares of Time Warner traded at
$33.50. If you see another number followed
by an "s" between the price and the symbol,

this means that a multiple of 100 shares was traded. TWX 5 s 33-1/2 means that 500 shares of Time Warner traded at $33.50.

HOW TO READ
MUTUAL FUND TABLES

NAV	Net Chg	Fund Name	Inv Obj	YTD %ret	4wk %ret	Total Return			Max Init Chrg	Exp Ratio
						1Yr-R	3Yr-R	%Yr-R		
Acme Funds										
9.07	+0.01	Bond	IB	-2.8	+0.7	+3.5E	+3.9D	+7.3D	4.00	1.03

Now that you've conquered stock quotations, let's move on to something even more critical for the average investor, reading mutual fund tables. Although the column headings are different, the basic logic is similar, so you shouldn't have much trouble understanding the tables if you read the following explanation.

NAV — This stands for Net Asset Value and is the value per share (calculated by dividing the total value of the fund by the number of shares outstanding).

Net Chg — Net Asset Value Change refers to the gain or loss experienced by the fund since the previous day's listing.

Fund Name — When it's in bold face, it's the name of the sponsoring company. Listed underneath, you'll find the names of the individual funds. For example, the famous Magellan Fund can be found by looking up Fidelity, its sponsoring company.

Inv Obj — This indicates the investment objective of the individual fund. In the case of this example, it's a bond fund. Other abbreviations include GR for growth, SC for small company stocks, and GI for growth and income. You'll find a key to these abbreviations along with the listings in your newspaper.

Total Return — This next major heading captures the net asset value change plus the income that the fund has accumulated for the period in question. The assumption is that all distributions have been reinvested. The capital letters after the entries show where the individual fund was ranked among similar funds for the time period. "A" means the stock was in the top 20 percent; "B" puts it in the next 20 percent, and so on.

Max Init Chrg — This very important number is the maximum initial sales commission that the fund charges. Funds with 0.00 in this column are no-loads, meaning that no commission is charged.

Exp Ratio — This means annual expenses, and is another critical number for investors seeking to maximize their returns. Expressed as a percentage of the value of your account, this indicates how much the fund charges you on an annual basis.

The Dow, S&P, and Leading Economic Indicators

THE KEY TO READING ANNUAL REPORTS

The look of annual reports tends to run in cycles like hemlines. During times of austerity and no-nonsense management, they tend to be lean and dry with few pictures and lots of graphs and charts. During times of economic expansion, annual reports are often lavish with lots of color photographs, ground-breaking graphic design and expensive paper. In general, experts will advise you to ignore the packaging and go straight to the back where you'll find the numbers and the CPA's report.

The CPA's or independent auditor's report is some of the most critical reading you'll do in an annual report. This will tell you whether or not the report was prepared according to "generally accepted accounting principles." If the accountant hedges at all, using language like "subject to" or "however" in respect to the company's financial statements, look out. This may mean that the company is trying to hide some bad news or create some good news with smoke and mirrors.

Another area that might tip you off about coming trends or soft spots in a company's operation is the letter from the chairman. It's usually found at the front of the report. The chairman's letter is supposed to be a straightforward explanation of how the business is doing. When the chairman waffles, and tells you something along the lines of "things would have been great if only something or another hadn't happened," this is another danger signal.

Now, on to the numbers. First, you should take a look at the balance sheet, which most experts refer to as a *snapshot* of a company's financial health. The balance sheet will contain the following categories:

Assets — This is everything that the company owns.

Current Assets — Liquid assets like cash or anything else that can easily be turned into cash.

Liabilities — Everything that the company owes including long-term and short-term debt.

Current Liabilities — These are the debts due within the coming year. Current liabilities will be paid out of current assets.

Working Capital — Reached by subtracting

current liabilities from current assets. Experts consider working capital to be a critical number, especially when it shrinks from one annual report to the next.

Stockholder's Equity — Subtract total liabilities from total assets and you'll get stockholder's equity. In a healthy company, this number will grow.

Long-Term Debt — Look at this number closely. If a company is growing rapidly and has taken on debt to finance the growth, you shouldn't worry. But a slow-growth company with heavy long-term debt is not a good investment prospect.

Income Statement — This number shows how much money the company made during the last fiscal year.

Net Earnings Per Share — There are so many ways to manipulate this figure that it's often hard to trust. A company can inflate its earnings in any given year by selling assets or by cutting their advertising budget. Either move may come back to haunt them and their stockholders in years to come.

Net Sales — Most experts consider this to be a more telling number. It indicates whether sales are keeping pace with (or outpacing) inflation, and whether sales are going up year after year. If net sales appear to be decreasing year after year, this could be a sign of trouble.

STOCK GURUS AND PUNDITS

For some reason, Americans have always loved a good huckster. Over the years we've embraced shady televangelists, real estate con men, political demagogues, pyramid schemers, and other get-rich-quick artists. Unfortunately, that also includes investment advisors who author some very pricey newsletters.

My father-in-law had one such fellow as a member of his congregation down in Florida. According to Reverend Smith, the man had a sweet nature and a nice bari-

INVESTMENT TIP #18

SOME MORE GOOD REASONS TO BUY STOCKS

Here's what experts like to see when deciding to invest in a company.

1. The company has a stockpile of cash over and above their need to pay dividends, reinvest in the company, or pay down debt.

2. When the company's P/E ratio is equivalent to its growth rate expressed in percentages. For example: Acme Corp. is growing at the rate of 16 percent annually and has a P/E ratio of 16.

3. The company makes a blockbuster of a product that represents a significant portion of sales. Example: Netscape and their Netscape Navigator for the Internet.

4. When a company with a strong equity position has very little long-term debt.

tone voice, which he used to great effect in the choir. Unfortunately, he also used that voice on the lecture circuit to persuade investors to "sell everything" when he was convinced the market was about to plummet, and to "buy like crazy" when he felt the market was about to soar. Like most prognosticators, he was right some of the time, but over the long haul, he was wrong more often than he was right. So, a word of caution when it comes to stock market gurus and the products they're selling: At the end of the day, there will be only one person making money, and it won't be you.

HOW TO MAKE SENSE OF THE DOW

When you hear Peter Jennings or Tom Brokaw report that the market was up by 6 points today, in all likelihood they're talking about the Dow Jones Industrial Averages, the oldest and most accepted indicator of the stock market's vitality.

What most people don't realize is that the Dow is a formula based on the stock prices of only thirty industrial companies.

All of the stock prices are added up and then divided by a special number to get the Dow Jones average. For the last hundred years, the Dow has been constructed pretty much the same way. Two senior editors from *The Wall Street Journal* pick the stocks based on how well they feel the companies represent the economy in general.

Great, you say, but how is the Dow useful to me as a small investor? Well, there are two ways in which you can use the Dow and similar market indexes, such as the Standard & Poor's 500. If you follow these models closely, you'll get a sense of whether the market is trending up or down. It's one major indicator of when it's time to buy and time to sell. Also, if the stocks in your portfolio tend to underperform the Dow and the market as a whole, then you might reconsider the value of holding onto them.

Clearly, the Dow is a great tool for market timers and momentum investors, but not everyone is enamored of it. Some investors fault the Dow because the companies in its portfolio are usually older; blue-chip corporations that don't always reflect the reality of the current economy. Others complain that the Dow Jones Averages focus too narrowly on current stock prices and fail to account for the overall value of the companies on the list.

Regardless of its shortcomings, the Dow is still the chief bellwether of Wall Street, and bears close watching—until someone comes along with something better.

HOW TO USE THE STANDARD & POOR'S 500

Although the S&P 500 is not as well-known to the average person as the Dow, savvy investors often prefer it as a tool to measure how well their portfolios are performing compared to the market. And they're not alone. The U.S. government includes the S&P 500 in their monthly report on the twelve leading economic indicators. They don't include the Dow.

The S&P 500 is different from the Dow

in several important ways. First, it's an index. It measures results against a standard point of reference in the past, rather than just averaging the prices of representative stocks today. Second, the Standard & Poor uses 500 stocks instead of 30, which S&P maintains is far more representative of the economy as a whole. Third, the stocks in the S&P are weighted according to how many shares a company has outstanding.

Just like the Dow, however, the stocks in the S&P 500 lean heavily toward New York Stock Exchange issues and tend to be older, well-established firms.

If you have a conservative portfolio, the S&P 500 might be a great tool to measure performance against. If you're more of a risk taker, who's invested heavily in new companies, you're probably better off consulting the NASDAQ index.

THE NASDAQ NATIONAL MARKET SYSTEM COMPOSITE INDEX

NASDAQ created an index in 1971 to monitor how well its stocks performed. Like the S&P 500, the NASDAQ Composite Index is weighted according to the number of shares of each stock that are outstanding. This index is a useful tool for investors who prefer higher risk investments.

ECONOMIC STATISTICS

If you've ever watched "Wall Street Week" or any of CNN's business coverage on television, you've undoubtedly heard commentators talk sagely about such things as the GNP, Housing Starts, and the Consumer Price Index. These are just a few of the economic statistics that professional investors follow in order to know where the economy is heading. Although average small investors shouldn't concern themselves with these indicators too much, they're still worth checking on periodically as a benchmark for the health of the economy. Listed below are a few of the indexes in which professional investors are most interested.

Gross National Product, or GNP, is the government's attempt to measure the value of all investments, consumer spending, and government spending in the United States. It's figured on a quarterly basis. Traditionally, when GNP figures come in much higher than Wall Street expects, professional investors worry about the economy overheating, and fear rising inflation. When the economy experiences two consecutive quarters of declining GNP, the government says the economy is in a recession.

Unemployment figures are also calculated by the government and watched closely by financial professionals. Paradoxically, when unemployment figures are low, they get worried again about rising inflation and start thinking about investing heavily in bonds rather than stocks.

The Money Supply is of interest to professional investors because all business activity is fueled by cash. If the Money Supply grows too slowly, business slows down, too. On the other hand, if the Money Supply grows too quickly, then inflation may begin to rise.

Once a month the government publishes the Index of Leading Economic Indicators, a list of twelve different economic statistics that, taken together, give investors a good snapshot of the economy. The twelve indicators include: average hours worked each week by workers in manufacturing; average number of first-time state unemployment claims; new orders received for consumer goods and materials; percentage of companies reporting a slowing of deliveries for things they've ordered; index of the net number of new businesses; the number of contracts signed and orders placed for new production facilities; building permits approved for new private housing; changes in manufacturing and trade inventories; changes in raw materials prices; changes in S&P 500; changes in money supply; and levels of consumer and business credit.

Professional investors tend to take the long view of all indexes, and so should you. If the Index of Leading Economic Indicators happens to show consistent declines over a period of months, then get concerned, but a single month's increase or decline is not considered anything noteworthy.

Getting the Straight Scoop

HOW TO FIND INFORMATION ON THE INTERNET

If your family is anything like mine, your home computer is currently being held hostage by the men and boys in the household. Rather than helping with homework and household accounting, our poor beleaguered Macintosh is forced to play endless games of Warcraft, Sim City 2000, and pay countless visits to the Nintendo home page on the Internet.

My advice: demand equal time! Recently, while Richard and the boys were away on a

Boy Scout outing, I discovered that the Internet is a fount of free information on investing. While my boys were sleeping in a pup tent in the village green, I was surfing the Net, discovering delightful places like *The Motley Fool*. It's an irreverent, but very useful investment forum found on America Online.

While you're on-line, you can hook up with discount brokers who offer special incentives to trade on-line, try new investment software, sample investment newsletters and other services, or visit Edgar, the Securities and Exchange Commission's very own website (http://www.sec.gov/edaux/current.htm*), and get current balance sheets for companies you're interested in.

But you should be careful about taking free advice. There's a lot of terrific information available on the Internet, but there's also a lot of dreck. Do your homework so you can tell which is which.

FORGET IT!

The worst place—bar none—to get information on investing is friends and relatives. If you're going to plunk down your hard-earned money on High Decibel Hard Drives just because Cousin Larry from Montauk tells you it can't miss, you might as well take your money to the racetrack. Believe me, you'll have a lot more fun losing it there.

Whenever you get an overwhelming urge to speculate on a stock because your intuition is working overtime or because of a hot tip, stop where you are. Then do the following things: go for a walk or jog to clear your head, and very carefully consider the source of the information that you have received. When my Uncle Max is making me crazy, I just picture him with a mouthful of chopped liver trying to whisper "garbage" in my ear. The urge to invest miraculously fades away.

If humor doesn't work for you, think about your sources logically. Do they really know more than professional investors? Are

INVESTMENT TIP #19

MONITORING YOUR INVESTMENTS BY COMPUTER

Apart from newspapers and on-line services, one of the best ways of keeping track of your investments is the personal computer. Whether you're a Macintosh aficionado or confirmed PC user, there are terrific software packages out there to help you analyze the performance of your investments quickly and easily— once you take the time to learn the software. Some packages like the popular Quicken will let you write checks and bank electronically, while others facilitate trading with discount brokers directly from your computer. Listed on the next page are just a few of the hundreds of software packages available.

they tapped in to the inner workings of the company in question?

INVESTMENT TRACKING SOFTWARE

Quicken
Intuit
Hardware: IBM, Macintosh
Price: $59.95

WealthBuilder by *Money* Magazine
Reality Technologies, Inc.
Hardware: IBM, Macintosh
Price: $69.95

Equalizer
Charles Schwab & Co., Inc.
Hardware: IBM
Price: $59; on-line fees additional

Fidelity On-line Xpress
Fidelity Investments
Hardware: IBM
Price: $49.95

Market Manager Plus
Dow Jones & Co., Inc.
Hardware: IBM, Macintosh
Price: $299 (30% AAII discount)

The fact is, there are no shortcuts to successful investing. You can't trust hot tips and you can't trust your gut instincts. You have to do your homework and carefully evaluate each security before you invest.

HOW TO KNOW WHEN TO BUY AND WHEN TO SELL

The difference between the average person and the smart investor is that the smart investor knows when to buy and when to sell. The smart investor ignores his or her emotions and lets the fundamentals dictate what to do.

The average person is ruled by emotions. He or she buys stocks when the market is at its peak and everyone is feeling prosperous, and sells when the market is down and everyone is feeling gloomy about the economy. And all the while the smart investor is doing just the opposite.

For instance, between October and December, a lot of investors, including institutions, tend to unload stocks that aren't doing well. They want to take the tax loss

INVESTMENT TIP #20

SAMPLING INVESTMENT NEWSLETTERS FOR FREE

Many experts believe that all investors should subscribe to one or more newsletters. There's quite a number of them to choose from and they cover anything you're apt to be interested in, from commodities trading to precious metals, global investing, and money markets.

If there's a topic that you're really interested in, you can get a free sample of a newsletter that covers the subject via the Internet. Next time you log on, visit The Newsletter Library at http://pub.savvy.com/subject.htm*. With 11,000 different newsletters, you're bound to get free samples on the subjects closest to your investment strategy.

INVESTMENT TIP #21

KEEP ABREAST OF THE NEWS

Whether you're part of the on-line community or just subscribe to a daily newspaper, you can do your portfolio a world of good just by staying on top of the news. If you're a long-term investor, you shouldn't be worrying too much about day-to-day fluctuations in your stock prices, but you should be concerned about company news that might affect performance and earnings. Watch especially for management changes, new product launches, or lawsuits. Many newspapers carry an index to companies in the business section, so when you look at the paper in the morning, get into the habit of checking the index for your companies.

and start clean in the new year. This end-of-the-year selling tends to depress prices across the board, creating opportunities for the smart investor with a well-researched shopping list. Bargains are also to be had after market corrections, such as the so-called crash of 1987. Instead of selling with the herd, savvy investors stuck around to pick up sound stocks at fire-sale prices.

But let's forget about the market for a minute. Unless they're market timers, savvy investors buy and sell on fundamentals and so should you. If your stock price has dropped and then stayed down for a number of months while the market remains strong, you should check the annual reports, the papers, and the Net. Talk with your financial advisor. If everything still seems strong, you might consider buying more while the prices are temporarily down.

But if the company's story has changed because of increased competition, declining profit margins, a high P/E ratio, or a sudden increase in debt due to acquisitions, then it's probably time to make a change in your portfolio.

YOUR SECRET WEAPON:
THE LIBRARY CARD

With a public library card you've got one of the most potent tools a small investor can have at his or her disposal. Not only can you find numerous books on investing, but you'll have ready access to newspapers and periodicals such as *The Wall Street Journal, Barrons, Fortune, Forbes, Business Week, Worth,* and *Money.* Furthermore, many libraries also subscribe to investment newsletters and services such as *The Value Line Investment Survey,* which many experts have compared to having your own stock market analyst on staff.

A word of caution: these publications are not in the investment business. They're in the journalism business. In other words, they make money by selling subscriptions and individual copies. Consequently, they are prone to manufacture stimulating headlines that often contain predictions about the future of the economy. Take these predictions with a grain of salt; they are often wrong!

INVESTMENT TIP #22

CHRISTMAS IN NOVEMBER, JUNE, OR JULY

If you've been making a Christmas list of stocks you'd like to own if they weren't so expensive, don't whisper them in Santa's ear. Wait until the year-end sell-off and see if some of your wish list doesn't drop in price. The key is to have a list ready before the market dips, whether it's because of year-end selling; or one of the periodic "corrections" the market goes through from time to time.

This doesn't mean the content of these publications is without value. You should read some of them regularly to find out what's happening in key industries and companies. You'll find out things about company management and personalities that could affect your investment decisions in a positive way.

So, if you don't already own a library card, apply for one today. As my father-in-law says, "If you can read and have a little patience, you can learn just about anything."

---

* All Worldwide Web addresses listed above were verified at printing time, however, these listings may change.

APPENDIX A

Index
of
Investment
Tips

APPENDIX B

Index
of
Helpful
Sidebars

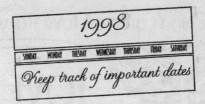

1998

SUNDAY   MONDAY   TUESDAY   WEDNESDAY   THURSDAY   FRIDAY   SATURDAY

Keep track of important dates

Three beautiful and colorful calendars that celebrate some of the most popular trends in America today.

Look for:

Just Babies—a 16 month calendar that features a full year of absolutely adorable babies!

> 1998 CALENDAR
> **Just Babies**
> 16 months of adorable bundles of joy!

> *Hometown Quilts*
> **1998 Calendar**
> A 16 month quilting extravaganza!

Hometown Quilts—a 16 month calendar featuring quilted art squares, plus a short history on twelve different quilt patterns.

Inspirations—a 16 month calendar with inspiring pictures and quotations.

> *Inspirations*
> A 16 month calendar that will lift your spirits and gladden your heart

Steeple Hill™

HARLEQUIN®

Value priced at $9.99 U.S./$11.99 CAN., these calendars make a perfect gift!

Available in retail outlets in August 1997.   CAL98

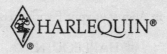

**HARLEQUIN AND SILHOUETTE
ARE PLEASED TO PRESENT**

Born in the USA

Love, marriage—and the pursuit of family!

Check your retail shelves for these upcoming titles:

July 1997
Last Chance Cafe by Curtiss Ann Matlock
The most determined bachelor in Oklahoma is in trouble! A
lovely widow with three daughters has moved next door—and
the girls want a dad! But he wants to know if their mom needs
a husband....

August 1997
Thorne's Wife by Joan Hohl
Pennsylvania. It was only to be a marriage of convenience—
until they fell in love! Now, three years later, tragedy
threatens to separate them forever and Valerie wants only to
be in the strength of her husband's arms. For she has some
very special news for the expectant father...

September 1997
Desperate Measures by Paula Detmer Riggs
New Mexico judge Amanda Wainwright's daughter has been
kidnapped, and the price of her freedom is a verdict in
favor of a notorious crime boss. So enters ex-FBI agent
Devlin Buchanan—ruthless, unstoppable—and soon there is
no risk he will not take for her.

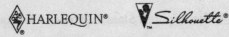

New York Times bestselling author

brings a love story that will take you...

ABOVE AND BEYOND

(previously published under the pseudonym Erin St. Claire)

Letters of love—to another man—brought them together. A powerful secret may tear them apart.

Trevor Rule fell in love with Kyla before he met her, just by reading the letters she'd written to her husband—Trevor's best friend. Now he had to convince Kyla that they both had the right to be happy and move past the tragedy of Trevor's death....

**Available in September 1997
at your favorite retail outlet.**

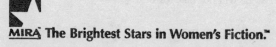

<u>MIRA</u> **The Brightest Stars in Women's Fiction.™**

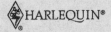

HARLEQUIN ULTIMATE GUIDES™

Act now to order more of these fabulously helpful books!

#80507	HOW TO TALK TO A NAKED MAN	$4.99 U.S. ☐ $5.50 CAN. ☐
#80508	I CAN FIX THAT	$5.99 U.S. ☐ $6.99 CAN. ☐
#80510	WHAT YOUR TRAVEL AGENT KNOWS THAT YOU DON'T	$5.99 U.S. ☐ $6.99 CAN. ☐
#80511	RISING TO THE OCCASION More Than Manners: Real Life Etiquette for Today's Woman	$5.99 U.S. ☐ $6.99 CAN. ☐
#80513	WHAT GREAT CHEFS KNOW THAT YOU DON'T	$5.99 U.S. ☐ $6.99 CAN. ☐
#80514	WHAT SAVVY INVESTORS KNOW THAT YOU DON'T	$5.99 U.S. ☐ $6.99 CAN. ☐

(quantities may be limited on some titles)

TOTAL AMOUNT $
POSTAGE & HANDLING $
($1.00 for one book, 50¢ for each additional)
APPLICABLE TAXES* $ _____
TOTAL PAYABLE $ _____
(check or money order—please do not send cash)

To order, complete this form and send it, along with a check or money order for the total above, payable to Harlequin Ultimate Guides, to: **In the U.S.:** 3010 Walden Avenue, P.O. Box 9047, Buffalo, NY 14269-9047; **In Canada:** P.O. Box 613, Fort Erie, Ontario, L2A 5X3.

Name: _____

Address: _____ City: _____

State/Prov.: _____ Zip/Postal Code: _____

*New York residents remit applicable sales taxes.
Canadian residents remit applicable GST and provincial taxes.

HARLEQUIN®